"In a world of permanent white water, the primary key to success is collaboration and co-creation; Katrin Muff provides us with a deep understanding of how to do what we most need to do."

—**Robert E. Quinn**, *Author of* Deep Change *and Cofounder of the Center for Positive Organizations at the University of Michigan*

"At last, a book for change-makers, innovators, and leaders from business, civil society, and governmental organizations that takes on the greatest change challenge of our day: *the polarization explosion*. While we have learned to deal with *classic conflict*, argues the brilliant Katrin Muff, today's *polarized conflict* is not only of a whole new magnitude but is of a different species of fracturing – where people are literally living in different realities pulling our societies and our most urgent change challenges apart.

"Moreover, this book is not about despair but hope, and it shows us *exactly how* to apply leading-edge research to propel new and inspiring vistas of co-creation. Written in an inviting style that is urgent, precise, and potent, Katrin Muff presents eye-opening stories from the field of how to traverse the arc from 'me' to 'we' and how to harness the *power of purpose* larger than the focal system – where 'recognizing multiple belongings creates bridges.' This book is for everybody who wants to make a difference at this time. It's for you, it's for me, and it's for everyone we know who wants to unleash the positive impact mindset."

—**David L. Cooperrider**, *Distinguished Professor and author of* The Business of Building a Better World

"This book outlines the mindset shift of leaders and organizations to innovate solutions for a sustainable and just world. The same mindset shift is much needed to overcome polarization. Katrin calls it the Positive Impact Mindset and her stories demonstrate how to use it. Highly recommended!"

—**Otto Scharmer**, *Senior Lecturer MIT and author of* Theory U

The Positive Impact Mindset

We are facing a new and urgent challenge when collaborating across organizations, and with broader stakeholder groups: how to overcome polarization. It has never been harder to find a common vision, when opinions are often considered as facts.

This book empowers change makers and business leaders to understand how successful organizations in the 21st century require leaders to become fluent in collaborating outside of traditional business boundaries. Such collaboration often involves working with parties that hold very different values, opinions, and priorities, and working with them requires new skills. Building on the book *Five Superpowers for Co-Creators*, Katrin Muff presents a number of real-world examples that demonstrate how organizations have successfully managed to address these challenges. Examples of such unlikely but successful cross-sector collaboration include a project addressing plastic waste in Switzerland, and two European city government projects that reached out beyond organizational boundaries. The book features many stories of trial and error in overcoming the societal polarization gap. From all these insights emerges clear guidance as to how leaders and organizations can transform to new "outside-in" mindsets to overcome polarization and develop a Positive Impact Mindset.

The book is ideal for use by facilitators, educators, business and political leaders, and consultants, who are seeking solutions within an often polarized world to achieve sustainable change and a positive impact.

Katrin Muff is a recognized thought leader in enabling leaders and organizations to see value in solving societal problems. Her facilitation solutions bridge sustainability and psychology. She combines two decades of global business experience with 15 years of academic leadership.

The Positive Impact Mindset

Working Together in a Polarized World

Katrin Muff

Routledge
Taylor & Francis Group
LONDON AND NEW YORK

Cover design: Jorge Scheurer

First published 2023
by Routledge
4 Park Square, Milton Park, Abingdon, Oxon OX14 4RN

and by Routledge
605 Third Avenue, New York, NY 10158

Routledge is an imprint of the Taylor & Francis Group, an informa business

British Library Cataloguing-in-Publication Data
A catalogue record for this book is available from the British Library

Library of Congress Cataloging-in-Publication Data
Names: Muff, Katrin, author.
Title: The positive impact mindset : working together in a polarized world / Katrin Muff.
Description: Abingdon, Oxon ; New York, NY : Routledge, 2023. | Includes bibliographical references and index.
Identifiers: LCCN 2022030153 (print) | LCCN 2022030154 (ebook) | ISBN 9781032306209 (hbk) | ISBN 9781032306230 (pbk) | ISBN 9781003305941 (ebk)
Subjects: LCSH: Organizational change. | Leadership. | Success in business.
Classification: LCC HD58.8 .M822 2023 (print) | LCC HD58.8 (ebook) | DDC 658.4/06—dc23/eng/20220909
LC record available at https://lccn.loc.gov/2022030153
LC ebook record available at https://lccn.loc.gov/2022030154

ISBN: 9781032306209 (hbk)
ISBN: 9781032306230 (pbk)
ISBN: 9781003305941 (ebk)

DOI: 10.4324/9781003305941

Typeset in Sabon
by Apex CoVantage, LLC

Contents

Figures

Figures

Preface

The future is created one room at a time, one gathering at a time. Each gathering needs to become an example of the future we want to create.

—*Peter Block*

The idea for this book was born out of a deep concern about the future of our societies. Not only has our ability to talk with each other dropped fast, distrust has become a new basic attitude. Distrust in government institutions, in mass media, and in those who hold a different opinion. My concern grew as I watched polarization explode in the United States during the Trump presidency. I saw polarization ignite and light up across Europe during the COVID-19 pandemic, and with great sadness I saw similar polarization as the Russian military invaded its neighboring country, the Ukraine. Polarization spreads like a wildfire burning down everything in its path, leaving democracies weakened and demagogues and autocrats strengthened. Divide and conquer, Julius Cesar had proclaimed two thousand years ago.

We need solutions to bridge the polarization that pulls our societies apart. With trust in government declining, people have new and larger expectations for the roles of business and nongovernmental organizations (NGOs). A global survey shows that government is considered incompetent and unethical, while business is considered competent and NGOs ethical. Business and NGOs are expected to provide societal leadership and a large majority of survey participants demands organizational leaders (CEOs) to personally engage in important societal topics.[1] If business and NGOs are to step up and their leaders are to embrace their positive role for society, they need to learn to deal with polarization.

I am a sustainability expert, and I dedicate my life to finding ways out of the dead end we have maneuvered ourselves into. For a long time, I related the notion of a dead end to the state of our planet and the damage we have inflicted on many of the planetary boundaries. This includes the climate emergency and our inability to flatten the curve of global carbon dioxide emissions in time to avoid climate disasters, such as floods, draughts, hail, rising sea levels, and extreme inhuman heat waves. More recently, the economic system has also showed signs of hitting a dead end. Weakened by the pandemic and shaken up by the Russian-Ukrainian war with its far-reaching consequences, global supply chain failures have disrupted local economies and have triggered famine and a global energy crisis. The related inflation and price hikes threaten low-income families globally. The rise of polarization has made me realize that our societies have now reached a dead end, too. Demagogues and autocrats are on the rise and the post-Cold War agreement of the rule of law has been shattered. We are dangerously close to a tipping point placing democracies in danger. Sustainability does include the environment, the economy, and society, and as a sustainability expert I am deeply concerned about the current and the future situation of all three of these dimensions.

This book focuses on the societal challenge caused by polarization and seeks to provide concrete solutions to overcome polarization so that a constructive dialogue among societal stakeholders is possible. We depend on these dialogues if we want to develop solutions to all three dimensions of the sustainability challenges. The underlying issues are of such complexity that no single institution can solve them in isolation. There are attempts at such dialogues across sectors, involving government, business, NGOs, and civil society, and a number of these dialogues result in constructive outcomes. Let us learn from what works and let us understand how to prevent and overcome hurdles and obstacles. This book is full of stories. Almost every chapter starts with one to illustrate either the challenges or a solution. The book also includes two in-depth case studies that demonstrate the challenges and the opportunities of such cross-sector collaboration involving government, business, and activists.

The insights and learnings in the book build on years of practice and research in the broad area of the Collaboratory methodology that was studied and enhanced in a series research initiatives called Leadership for Transition (LiFT), which were funded by the European Union (EU). The Collaboratory methodology was initially designed for one-day multistakeholder conversations and thereafter expanded to the comprehensive stakeholder co-creation approach consisting of multiple building blocks. In this next iteration, we have explored how to integrate the political sphere and the related complex decision-making processes. We have studied multiple situations of failure and success and reflected on the emerging insights from an integral perspective – all of this to learn how to enable a suitable dialogue among government, business, civil society, leaders, and change makers. This dialogue is essential to address and resolve the sustainability challenges we face despite the divergent interests of the involved parties.

Polarization has raised conflicts to a next level of complexity. While we have learned how to deal with classic conflicts, we will now need to learn how to deal with polarized conflicts. This book offers a suggested pathway to do so. Polarized conflicts require a new initial step before two opposed parties are able to sit together. This step is about creating a human connection as a foundation to rise above the different realities the polarized parties inhabit. Solving polarized conflicts requires moving from the transactional thinking that is used to resolve classic conflicts to a transformational thinking. Instead of settling for a win-win solution that suits the parties involved, overcoming polarized issues and solving our global, complex challenges require the involved parties to embrace a shared, higher purpose. This requires a transformation in thinking. Such a thinking requires an introspection regarding our own mindset. The book provides leading-edge research insights on such a mindset transformation. We differentiate between the individual mindset of leaders and change makers and the organizational mindset of the institutions they represent. The transformation is about overcoming the traditional egocentric, competitive worldview to embrace a higher-purpose vision that is developed in a co-creative approach. The transformation journey is outlined in all available detail and enriched with stories. It builds on ground-breaking scientific work and is complemented with research insights from other fields. The goal is to make the insights accessible for a layman audience.

My ambition was to write a highly readable short book for change makers and business leaders of all types of organizations including government and business. Such leaders need to collaborate with other-minded people to achieve a positive impact for society. I have approached the topic in four steps, which I have used to structure the book. Part I describes the challenges of a polarized society and how this creates a new level of complexity when collaborating with others. Part II compares the transactional approach of classic conflicts with the transformational perspective required to solve polarized conflicts and identifies transferable insights from other fields. Part III studies the underlying mindset transformation and unpacks the related challenges at the level of an individual leader and an organizational mindset. Part IV completes the lessons learned with additional stories and research insights, and ends with plenty of recommendations.

When I started this book project, I tentatively called it "Changing Minds in a Polarized World." As I started researching, I had to admit that changing minds was possibly overambitious as a goal. I reminded myself that we can only really change our own mind. As a result, I amended the title to "Opening Minds in a Polarized World," thinking that it would at least be a fine goal to be able to sit together and create a space where all parties would engage in a dialogue and walk away with an opened mind. I started to interview people for stories and found out that the reality was different and that polarization had a strong impact on how open or closed our minds are. In my personal life, I faced situations with friends that made me understand that opening minds was not always an option. During a long walk with a close friend who was on the other side of the COVID-19 measures, I suggested that we could focus on keeping a dialogue open and that it appeared important to keep building bridges. This was the one thing we agreed on. And that is why my book title evolved to "Building Bridges in a Polarized World." Focusing my book on my target audience, the change makers of this world, I reckoned that "Working Together in a Polarized World" would actually be more concrete and realistic. It was, after all, about working together. My editor, James Jesserer, helped me understand that the world has in fact moved on and that things are more dire now, suggesting that "Surviving in a Polarized World" would capture the spirit and the challenge of our times most accurately. Ultimately, my editor Rebecca Marsh suggested highlighting the solution in the title and therefore "The Positive Impact Mindset" was born, moving the previous title to its subtitle.

I hope this book creates the necessary awareness, understanding, and concrete tools to address and overcome polarization such that we can again work together to create a world worth living in. For this, a flexible mind and an open heart are of essence, as we will need to be willing to have conversations that will change us. Or, as Otto Scharmer, co-founder of the Presencing Institute, has so adequately put it: "Nobody has come out of a good conversation unscathed." May you have many, many such good conversations.

Rome and Luzern, Summer 2022

Note

1 The 2022 Edelman Trust Barometer: www.edelman.com/trust/2022-trust-barometer

Acknowledgements

I feel deeply grateful to be able to write. It has become an important part of my life and has deepened my relationship with the world, the society I live in, the people around and myself. Being gifted time to write is an incredible privilege that I treasure dearly.

In this sense, a big thank you to the Leadership in Transition (LiFT) team and in particular to Elke Fein and Bettina Geiken for your continued belief, trust and encouragement in my work. This book would not exist without you!

The insights of this book were developed in many conversations and through many stories. I am very grateful for your willingness to publicly share yours. Thank you Berit Ann Roos, Bernard LeRoux, Patricia von Lanthen, Simone Alabor, Suzie Scott, Tanja Mächler-Diethelm and Walter Fassbind. The book also builds on important scientific insights that have enriched my thinking during the intense year of research and reading. Thank you in this context Anne Caspari.

Writing a book in a language that is not your own is a nerve-wracking exercise. Thank you, James Jesserer, for the incredible labor of love of having edited the first draft of the book. This was a game changer for me as it allowed me to read my own words with a bit less embarrassment and more joy. I am forever grateful, brother! Thank you, Rebecca Marsh, for your continued support and your guidance as an editor. You have been with me all along and I am incredibly grateful for this third book with you!

Thank you, Jorge Scheurer, for helping me wrap my head around the cover page. It was a journey!

And – definitely not last – thank you my partner in life, Thomas Dyllick, for your patience and for your support. For waiting when I said "just a few more minutes" and it would take another hour. For cooking amazing meals and for being along cross-country skiing, hiking, walking, swimming and any other important distraction, when we needed a break from writing!

Thank you!

Part I

A new level of complexity

Part I explores how polarization impacts our ability to work and collaborate together. Polarization in society has increased immensely in the past years. There are a number of factors that have contributed to this increase: In certain countries, it has been caused by topics in the political arena, in others it became obvious as a result of the COVID-19-related measures, sometimes it is triggered by a blatant propaganda of disinformation, and often it is amplified through social media algorithms.

We explore how this rise of polarization results in divergent realities and what this does to our ability to work together. Polarized conflicts are of a different nature than classic conflicts. Satisfying the principal interests of both parties to reach a win-win situation will not work. In a polarized conflict, the parties live in different realities and are likely to refuse to even talk to each other, as they reject the reality of the other party.

The in-depth analysis of the Swedish hospital case provides insights into how a polarized conflict can be addressed and what new challenges emerge as a result. The case study highlights how the polarized parties can find a way to collaborate. In our uncertain and complex times, we will need to find approaches to collaborate effectively across sectors and we shall notice an increase in collaboration of government, business, NGOs, and civil society to resolve the burning issues of our planet, our societies, and our economies. Each of these institutions brings different experiences, expectations, and perspectives to the table, many of which can easily trigger a classic or a polarized conflict. How can we collaborate in such a situation? How do we keep connected when talking becomes impossible? The selected short stories offer insight into the complexity of polarized situations. If you are part of a multistakeholder collaboration or are likely to become a part of such processes, it is important that you are

DOI:10.4324/9781003305941-1

aware of the types of situations you might face and what you can do to overcome them.

Classic conflicts occur between parties that share the same reality. Polarized conflicts occur between people who live in different realities. Classic conflicts can be resolved using traditional conflict resolution methods. For polarized conflicts, creating a space where both parties can experience a human connection becomes a pre-condition for resolving the conflict. Part I creates the awareness for the difference of classic versus polarized conflicts and outlines the importance of overcoming polarization so that we can work together effectively.

1 Polarization greatly expands conflict

Short story: a polarized Russian-Ukrainian household

Svetlana is in a tough spot. Her husband, Volodya, and her older son have fully bought into the propaganda drummed into them by the Kremlin about the situation in the Ukraine. They call the Ukrainians Nazis and traitors and accuse the West of blindly believing the fake news provided by the Ukraine. Svetlana was born in the south of the Ukraine and came to Moscow in her twenties. She met Volodya in Moscow. Since the start of the war, she has tried calling her friends in the Ukraine, but nobody answers their phone. She hopes that they can reconnect again after everything has calmed down. She is clearly worried about what happens in the Ukraine, but she is even more worried about what happens in her home.

Svetlana is mostly concerned about holding her own family together. Her younger son who studies Chinese and wants to become a teacher is critical of Russia and says there is no hope for the country anymore. At 23 years old, he wonders if there will ever be a job for him in Russia and if he will be free to teach what he thinks is right. He says Russians will be back in the same situation as in 1937, and he rejects the propaganda forcefully. The arguments in Svetlana's home have caused great damage. Volodya spends most of his time at a cafe around the corner, catching up with the state news. He is concerned about repairing his truck, which he needs for work. There are no more spare parts. The family has grown silent, they have stopped watching television together, as each news bulletin is cause for a new conflict.

All that Svetlana wants is peace in her own house. She says that she did not bring two sons into this world to lose them over a fight. She cannot afford an opinion of her own and is at a loss of how to

DOI:10.4324/9781003305941-2

keep the family together. For the moment, not talking about things and not watching TV appears to work – but for how long?

In early April 2022, Silke Bigalke visited the family in Moscow and reported about it in the Swiss news.[1] She describes a typical polarized situation. The father and the older son live in one reality, the mother and the younger son in another. Under no circumstances is it possible to bridge the perspectives. Imposing silence on the topic is the only thing that appears to work. The tension is, however, palpable and it is likely that, over time, the conflict will burst out into the open again. The polarization in this case is about the Ukrainian war and is caused to a large degree by the Russian media, which reports an increasingly partial and distorted perspective. Many of us have experienced polarization in our families or circle of friends in recent times, too. COVID-19 has contributed much to the spreading of polarization beyond the political division. Many of us have experienced the effect of different sources of news and the unbridgeable, separate realities this creates.

The rise of polarization

There is a connection between the rise of polarization and the weakening of democracies around the world. Polarization has not just weakened democratic nations; it has also resulted in democracies around the world to be weakened. In March 2022, when the United Nations (UN) General Assembly approved a resolution that suspended Russia's membership in the UN Human Rights Council, a surprising number of countries either abstained or voted against the resolution. In fact, only 53% of the nations present approved the resolution, a sobering moment for our humanity. Of the 58 nations that abstained their vote and the 24 nations that voted against the suspension of Russia, most are located in Central Asia and Africa. However, South and Central American countries like Brazil, El Salvador, Nicaragua, and Mexico, as well as India and Indonesia, have abstained from voting. Countries like China, Cuba, Bolivia, Iran, and Vietnam were among the nations that voted against Russia's suspension. When adding in the 18 absent countries, a total of 100 nations refused to acknowledge the blatantly obvious war crimes of Russia in the Ukraine. This is a most troublesome picture of the state of the world.

Democracy is neither the dominant nor the steadfast backbone of humanity. Furthermore, polarization further contributes to weakening our old and strong democracies, such as the United States, where the political rift has further deepened during the Trump presidency. Moreover, Europe is not in great shape. In Germany, for example, Alternative for Germany has an extremist right wing, which is in the hard grip of conspiracy theorists.

What is the cause of polarization and why has it spread so easily in the past decade?

Analyzing global trust as a result of the COVID-19 pandemic provides an indication of the growth of polarized conflicts versus classic conflicts. With more than six million lives lost and a degree of joblessness that is equivalent to the Great Depression in the 1930s, trust has eroded around the world. The 2021 global trust barometer published annually by Edelman points to the size of the challenge we face.[2] Citizens trust their own governments less than before the pandemic. This lack of trust in governments and continued lack of trust in media have driven trust to a record low. A particular concern are those people who do not check their sources to ensure credible and factual information before it is shared. The perspectives of these people will impact society negatively, as we have observed with such doubters being substantially less willing to be vaccinated than those with good information hygiene. By 2022, distrust has become the new default around the globe.[3]

Hany Farid, a professor at the University of California, Berkeley, unpacks the myth around the info-demic. He differentiates between misinformation and disinformation. Misinformation is often shared by clueless people who believe that the information they share is true. They are simply misinformed and develop a stubborn resistance against science. Disinformation is generated and shared with the purpose to mislead readers. Hany Farid conducted a global study assessing the basic knowledge about COVID-19 by means of 20 questions that were clearly wrong and 20 questions that were correct. The depth and breadth of disinformation in societies across the world is baffling. Twenty percent of people around the world believe that Bill Gates sought to implant them with a microchip via the COVID-19 vaccination. These results were true irrespective of age, gender, level of education, or geographic region.[4] Hany Farid concluded that we are much dumber than we think we are. Indeed, the mind is a strange place and we need to acknowledge and accept that particularly after COVID-19, there is a certain percentage of people who no longer believe what they read on mainstream media and from official sources including science. This is our today's reality – like it or not.

Twisted social media algorithms provide a further part of the answer. They create very effective bubbles where users spend time nearly exclusively with those who share their opinions. Algorithms ensure that any news that pop up match with our opinion and hence reinforce our thinking and confirm our worldview. Over time, this can easily result in us believing to live in one kind of a reality, while people who think differently live comfortably in their own reality. Often, these two groups go about their separate lives without any real exposure to each other. This results in suspicions being steadily confirmed and vindicated. The more users read, the most knowledgeable and up to date they assume they are and the more right they believe they are. Social media helps amass further evidence amounting to incredible amounts of detailed information about a given subject. The information is filtered to suit initial prejudices and the user is mostly ignorant if such information is fake or real.

In comparison to this online world, I recall the good old times when our local newspaper featured opinions from the full spectrum of political opinions, implicitly seeking to provide a balanced perspective to its readers. It sounds like a utopia. We no longer have a common media that endorses different political positions. Each perspective has its own media and, hence, lives in its own world. Polarization is the visual result of parallel realities that now exist.

Divergent realities

When people with different opinions live in parallel realities, they no longer co-exist and can no longer acknowledge each other's opinions. Such societies become polarized and often bitterly politicized. We can observe this in large parts of the Western world, in North America, and in Europe. A healthy democracy, however, depends on the ability of all parties to negotiate and to reach a compromise, to resolve conflicts, and to accept and respect different opinions.

What is the impact of such polarization? In 2021, a majority of German citizens believe they are being bossed around, that they are being manipulated and somehow diminished in their rights by the dominant view of the cultural elite and the government. This is an important change to a decade earlier. In 2010, two thirds of surveyed Germans stated that they felt free. Most recently, however, only 45% of Germans feel that they can freely express their opinion, with 44% disagreeing. Members of the growing right-wing Alternative for Germany feel the most restrained and diminished. It is mostly those who do not like immigration, Islam, homosexuality, and gender-adjusted language who complain. They feel reduced to being treated as racists, sexists, and dull hillbillies by the mainstream media.

More and more topics are perceived as being delicate, for example, not just the subject of immigrants and the Islamic threat but also patriotism and equal rights. A majority of Germans believe that it is better to be careful when expressing opinions on these topics, as undesired opinions are socially punished. In fact, 71% of Germans complain about the restrictions set by gender-appropriate language, which they think is exaggerated. A large majority believe that they can no longer express themselves freely, that they are being ganged up on. Additionally, 55% of participants confirm that they purposefully refuse to express themselves in a politically correct manner because they are annoyed that others try to impose language rules on them.[5]

This sentiment is connected to more and more journalists refusing to remain objective. When the *New York Times* fired Bari Weiss, she became instantly famous. She had criticized the activism of younger journalists and had suggested that publishing houses prohibit their staff from using Twitter.[6] Her speaking up was unusual, as she belongs to the rainbow alliance of the elite. She mirrors the sentiment of Germans, i.e., that opinions can no longer be expressed freely. Weiss points out that a new ideology has replaced the liberalism of the old times. This new ideology focuses on an identity politics, which results in certain opinions being desired and others being labeled as not acceptable. She describes the inner reflection process of the *New York Times* after the unexpected election of Trump as president in 2016. The newspaper had propagated that Hilary Clinton would win with a degree of certainty of 99% and was seriously shaken by how wrong they had been. To increase the intellectual diversity, they invited people like Bari Weiss to join the newspaper. Notwithstanding, they could not integrate such diverse thought. Weiss's opinions stood in too much contrast to that of the rest of the in-house journalists. Weiss believes that the 2020 Black Lives Matter movement has confirmed a dangerous development among younger journalists: They no longer want to report neutrally; they want to ensure that they stand on the right side of history. This attitude is contrary to the traditional understanding of journalism.

This is an interesting effect of polarization. It shows that polarization has overshadowed classic conflict. Conflict no longer occurs between the shared reality of two different worldviews; it now highlights two very different realities, both of which exclude and deny the other's existence. When two realities exist, there is no longer a common basis for discussion. Such is the new reality of polarized conflict.

All of these different bubbles are an important part of what makes it so difficult to find agreement among those of different opinions. It takes a broader view, a step back from one's position, to see the bigger picture. This is easier said than done. Contextualizing our worldview is challenging enough; contextualizing our very existence, the reality we believe in, may well be too much to ask for. It takes a mindset transformation to achieve this, a shift from an ego-centric to an eco-centric view as Otto Scharmer would say. Exploring this challenge with an integral perspective, the challenge is about changing from the individual level to the collective level. On the individual level, we consider worldviews and values and when these do not match with the person we debate against, the worldviews and values are in competition. When moving up to the collective level, we step above personal worldviews and focus on shared values and a shared purpose. A shared purpose enables individuals to align with issues and agreements that are only partially represented by their individual-level worldviews. This is the space where agreements can be made. Yet, how do we progress from the individual to the collective level and how do we find such agreement?

Notes

1 Bigalke, S. (2022): Stimmen aus der Parallelwelt. *Tagesanzeiger*, April 6, accessed online April 8, 2002: https://epaper.tagesanzeiger.ch/article/20/20/2022-04-06/4/127803604?signature=539bdef01158149e0e55a88bf57c667842b87b3279a135fe16bc7ce8cd619235
2 The 2021 Edelman Trust Barometer: www.edelman.com/trust/2021-trust-barometer
3 The 2022 Edelman Trust Barometer: www.edelman.com/trust/2022-trust-barometer
4 Langer, M.-A. (2021): We are much dumber than we like to think. *NZZ*, August 17: www.nzz.ch/english/social-media-spreads-misinformation-berkeley-researcher-says-ld.1638804
5 Eigenmann, D. (2021): Die Mehrheit der Deutschen fühlt sich gegängelt. *Tagesanzeiger*, June 24, accessed online July 4, 2021: https://epaper.tagesanzeiger.ch/#article/20/Tages%2DAnzeiger/2021-06-24/4/123611291
6 Gasteiger, C., and Mayer, V. (2021): Immer mehr Journalisten wollen nicht objektiv sein. *Tagesanzeiger*, March 30, accessed online July 4, 2021: https://epaper.tagesanzeiger.ch/#article/20/Tages%2DAnzeiger/2021-03-30/12/121408279

2 A practice case – polarization in society

Case study: the Swedish hospital – a new type of conflict

In a region of Sweden, activists occupied the foyer of a local hospital when the local government announced plans to close down the hospital's maternity section. The particular region has a long history of protest reaching back to forest barons buying up the land, causing a prevailing rich-versus-poor resentment. When the government decided to close down the maternity section of that region, the outcry was immense. The consequence of the closure was disastrous for families, as pregnant women would have to travel a considerable distance for large parts of the year in dangerous, icy conditions to reach the next larger hospital. The occupation lasted two years without the government intervening. The government took a position of not wanting to give the activists any form of legitimacy by entering into discussions with the activist. Also, the government had never imagined that the activists would manage to organize themselves so well into an around-the-clock hospital occupation. The conflict resulted in the governing party losing many votes in the next regional election. The incoming premier had promised the people that he would resolve the conflict by entering into a dialogue with the activists.

The new premier reached out to the Association for Local Authorities and Retentions, who, in turn, tasked a professional mediation group to arrange the promised dialogue. The mediators' approach was that the activists needed to be involved directly in a face-to-face dialogue. Reaching out to local associations for help in this was another unprecedented major step. In Sweden, governments, once elected, often proceed with a clear sense that they have received a mandate to govern. At best, they have consultations with the citizens, but real collaboration is not the norm. The activists were skeptical and did not trust the

DOI:10.4324/9781003305941-3

promise that the government would truly listen. The activists' activities had been labeled as illegal and they were, by implication, considered as criminals. The activists did not trust the government at all.

The mediators travelled for several weeks back and forth between the government office and the hospital further inland for the purpose of convincing the two parties to sit down in the same room. The built-up mistrust and disrespect on both sides was significant. The tone on social media was characterized by personal attacks, making a face-to-face meeting a near impossibility. The mediators set up a kind of a pre-deal prior to the first meeting. The pre-deal consisted of parties agreeing to certain rules of engagement. These rules of engagement were needed, given there was a great deal of skepticism at first on the part of the activists. They did not trust that the conversation would be for real and suspected the regional government of simply suggesting dialogue for show. When asked what they wanted, the activists explained that the conversation had to lead to real change and that they wanted the government to be serious about bringing about change. The facilitators conveyed this to the government. The participating government members agreed that they would be open but could not promise specific changes in advance. The government representatives believed that they did not wish the tone of the meeting to be aggressive and suggested that both parties agree in advance to listen and allow the other side to speak. With these safety measures in place, the two parties agreed to meet face to face. The pre-dialogue contact also served to establish trust in the process and in the neutrality of the mediators.

This case was contributed by Bernard le Roux, one of my colleagues of the Leadership for Transition (LiFT) project. The project studies how multistakeholder processes can effectively work across a variety of societal settings, now including also the political dimension.

Case analysis

This case is interesting, as it highlights the age-old division of a rich versus poor worldview. There are ageless stories of the type of Robin Hood who stands up for the poor and acts against the law in place. Current societal conditions are considered unfair for the minority that needs to be defended, and breaking the law is justified by protecting the poor. What is clear is that in such situations these opposing resentments are so important that it is no longer possible to sit across a table and find an agreement. The worldviews originate in a very different perception of reality, if not in entirely different realities.

What this case demonstrates is how there is a need for a first step before the opposing parties can meet to explore potential solution. There is a need for a human connection, which then enables the re-creation of a foundation of trust on which bridges can be built. This case also shows how easily such trust can be lost again. Let us study at a more granular level how the mediators attempted to create this all-important human connection without which polarized conflict cannot be addressed.

The mediators had succeeded in creating a foundation of trust such that both the government and activist representatives could meet. They created a foundation for opposing parties could meet to resolve an issue both cared about and both needed to see solved (in Chapter 11 we refer to this as an issue alliance). Both parties met with a desire to communicate their convictions and to resolve the issue to their own satisfaction. The first meeting kicked off in a very tense atmosphere. People shifted around uneasily and did not know how to talk to each other. During the initial long check-in where each participant took a turn in expressing why they were there, the tension diminished considerably. The simple fact of speaking out about what was happening reduced the stress that was palpable in the room. Everybody appeared to be figuring out if and to what degree they could trust the process and those on the other side.

At one point, there was a flare up where one side accused the other of personal attacks on social media, which they said was simply unacceptable. The tension immediately rose again in the room. The mediators opted to stay with the topic, creating a space for those involved on both sides to resolve the issue. The mediators realized that these social media posts were a major source of the tension between the two sides, and the two individuals who argued understood that they would need to work together to lower the tone on social media and agree to a certain conduct whereby there would be no further personal attacks for the duration of the negotiations. Both groups agreed to ensure that their side would lower the tone on social media.

This small success of a first joint agreement in service of solving the shared issue brought about a turning point. It demonstrated to everybody in the room that agreements could be made and that decisions in the interest of both sides could be reached. Often, small steps like this create big transformations in the energy in a room. Suddenly, there was more informality in the room. The parties started joking and the atmosphere lifted considerably. First inklings of personal relationships started to develop among people who had previously never before spoken directly with each other. An early sign of success was when a member of the one party asked a member of the other party if it was acceptable for them to contact each other in between the dialogue sessions to try and keep the social media under control. These connections are important signs of early, fragile trust.

In the third meeting, the two sides started to agree on a set number of issues and they agreed that they would engage in a longer process to solve a number of the underlying conflicts. While the regional government was reluctant to agree to the re-opening of the maternity section, they said that they would consider speaking about other issues that were important to the activists. For example, the local government agreed to include the citizens in a process where the decision would be made to re-open the surgery section – a requirement for a maternity ward to exist. While activists regarded these as steps in the right direction, they would, however, continue their occupation until such time as their demands were resolved. The two sides also agreed that they would together investigate the staffing of the maternity and surgical sections and together find means of attracting qualified nurses and doctors to the rural hospital.

Unfortunately, as the planned broader dialogue with staff, officials, politicians, and other stakeholders started up, the regional government decided that they wanted to assume control of the process. They no longer required the services of the mediators. As a result, many of the activists lost trust in the process and the dialogue stopped. Both parties retreated back to their defensive positions. There is talk about restarting the conversation with more stakeholders, new moderators, and a new trust-building exercise.

This case is interesting, as it shows the highs and lows – the true challenges – of attempting to bring together parties that are divided in a polarized conflict. There is much to learn from this case.

Case learnings

The case provides a rich contextual setting for our current reality of having to work across sectors to address the complex problems we face. Government, civil society, and business are challenged to find approaches to bridge the often-significant differences in perspectives and worldviews. If we want to find means to address the health crisis that emerges when a pandemic strikes, the crisis resulting from an economic slowdown, or the climate crisis, we need to learn how to deal not just with a classic conflict but also with a polarized conflict. The key learning from this case is that a polarized conflict requires an initial step that precedes the resolution of a classic conflict. The involved parties need to first find a common human connection that is strong enough to overcome the different realities the parties live in and from which they see the world. The human connection provides the basis of trust and respect and enables – when successful – a bridge such that the parties can see each other. This "seeing another" is a basis for a broader reality that allows parties with different realities to open up and listen to another – and from here on, we can apply classic conflict resolution methods, which we explore later in the book.

In hindsight, persuading the opposing parties to sit down together in the room at all costs was part of the reason why the talks ultimately failed. The gap between the experience of a government that just does not listen, and the suggestion of a dialogue was too big and the bridge across the gap was not solid enough. It turned out that the government's complex multi-party structure did not allow it to keep the approach of a process where parties speak with each other on equal terms. The premier did not have the power to make that happen, as his party did not govern alone but in a coalition with an opposing party. When the mediators had reached out to the various government representatives, they did not succeed in making them fully understand and accept that the process of reaching agreements and making peace would require sharing power to a certain extent with the citizens. Resolving complex societal conflicts requires moving away from the hierarchical control that governments on a local and regional level are accustomed to in Sweden. The mediators also failed to recognize the importance of ensuring that internal dissent is dealt with in advance and not – as was the case here – allowed to sabotage agreements that had been reached.

This specific insight in the working of government was noted as a further major learning for the mediators; it highlights how complex the collaboration within and with government truly is. A government is not a business with a clear leader; it is a multi-player coalition created for a limited period of time that operates on untransparent rules which are fluid depending on both the persons in play and the issues at stake. In Chapter 11, we refer to this as a market partnership, highlighting that the solution can still be achieved within the same mindset, given that a part of the conflict is of a classic nature with all parties operating from the same worldview and referring to the same reality. The case illustrates the complexity of conflict resolution in the public sphere where engaged citizens, business, and politicians are forced to work together.

Last but not least, the case study teaches just how hard it is for somebody to change her or his mind if she or he is afraid of losing control of the process. In the case study, there was much at stake for both sides. If the activists agreed to open the hospital doors, how could they be assured that they would retain any control over the hospital? Retaining control was vital for the activists to maintain a negotiation leverage. Furthermore, if the government officials chose to override the local medical department by bringing in external citizens in decision-making processes that had traditionally been entirely owned by the government, how could the government officials ensure that they would not lose control of their processes. The fear of losing control and of things moving beyond control turned out to be major stumbling blocks that could not be overcome by either side of the negotiation table.

Conflicts are hard, and even harder when involving multiple stakeholders. Conflicts burst into an entirely other type of conflict when different realities cause polarized positions. At this point, we pause to state that we have not yet reached the stage of studying how to resolve such conflicts; at this juncture, we investigate cases to understand the difference between classic and polarized conflict. This approach is followed to assess how to best solve both of these aspects with the appropriate means. In Part II, we explore how to solve both classic and polarized conflicts.

3 The challenge of finding agreement

Short story: James and the meta-level challenge

James is the former international sales director of a sporting goods company. He is American and is married to a German. As a result, he commutes between the United States and Germany, often travelling to visit his aging mom back home. The COVID-19 pandemic reinforced the fault line of the political division among his siblings. Only, in this case the disagreement about the severity of the disease impacted their mom. The siblings disagreed widely about who could visit their mom and whether protective masks had to be worn or not. Worst of all, their mom became infected by COVID-19 and passed away. This only increased the division among the siblings and hardened the fault line. Looking back, James says: "Take family history, throw it in a shaker full of polarization, add a dash of emotion and you have the recipe for a tasty stew of a really great drama!"

James analyzes the division among his siblings and families in general. He has observed that during family reunions, such as Thanksgivings, family relationships would often be "frozen" to survive the holidays. By frozen he means that people would "wall off" and not address issues and avoid difficult conversations. There would be clearly denoted zones that were off limits for conversation. For him, this means that there is no opportunity for growth, and no opportunity to grow either the individual or the collective awareness. James compares the growing polarization to a black hole, saying: "Remember, a black hole itself is invisible, it can only be observed by the radiation it emits." The black-hole metaphor is well-fitting as it highlights the damage that polarization, instead of the issue itself, causes.

DOI:10.4324/9781003305941-4

Evaluating himself critically, James observes that there are two perspectives to consider. He calls them two angels. The better angel in him has him focus on the goodness and the decency of the other person. It encourages him to focus on true listening. Nevertheless, he is also familiar with the darker angel that has him focus on the toxic, lethal elements leading to further estrangement. This is the angel – or perspective – that puts relationships at risk. James is unsure how to engage positively with people who are unable or unwilling to see the world beyond a black and white lens, filtering out all the nuances. Married a second time, James is no stranger to relationship challenges; all successful relationships require compromise. He suggests that compromise has become a dirty word. If only one side compromises, there is resentment. A true compromise consists of neither party obtaining everything they wanted. This, he says, is an easily accepted truth in business negotiations but not in personal life and not in politics. To James, this professional conduct that used to exist at least to a certain degree in the political landscape, has disappeared in recent years – not the least due to the negative role modeling of former President Trump.

This story plays again at the individual, family level. Importantly, we need to acknowledge that we as individuals are the starting base of any change. The story is interesting, as it shows that James confuses the transactional perspective that dominates in business with the transformational approach required to resolve polarized conflicts. As a salesman, he is used to the dominant transactional perspective in business. We call it win-win. We focus on what is of key importance to each party, we all give up a bit of what we can let go of, and then we can find a deal that works for both parties. This approach works well in classic conflicts, and it fails easily in polarized conflicts.

A polarized conflict requires the involved parties to agree on a shared higher purpose from which a new solution can be found in service of such a higher cause. This may mean that one or both parties need to give up their positions. This is only possible when there is a higher purpose that both parties perceive as being worth enough to abandon an important principle. Furthermore, both parties need to recognize that their perspective is not the entire truth. The more difficult this is, the more likely it is that the parties face a polarized conflict.

Personal rights versus common interest

Let us consider the implications of polarized realities and the need for a meta-level perspective in the context of solving complex problems. Solving complex problems requires the involvement of different stakeholders, as no single perspective can unpack the issues or identify the solution. What this means is that stakeholders with different realities will need to align their perspectives to find a common agreement. The COVID-19 pandemic has highlighted a number of the underlying issues of polarization. At this juncture, we study the conflicting perspectives of personal freedom versus a civic responsibility.

COVID-19 has also been a magnifying glass pointing out the conflict of personal interest versus assuming a civic duty; it has revealed the attitude of people in our societies in times of uncertainty. The biological health threat reduced us to our existential behavior. The global nature of the pandemic implied that the attitude we assume when dealing with the virus is not only a private matter. Richard David Precht suggested that our attitude toward COVID-19 represents not only an ethics of living but also an ethics of living together. The consequences of the pandemic confronted us with our rights and responsibilities. For many members of Western societies this was the first time that they have experienced such restrictive impositions by a state. Unsurprisingly, such behavioral prompts triggered resistance. There was a growing sentiment that the request to do one's duty as a citizen is rooted in fascism or dictatorship. Even if, of course, the aforementioned request is rooted in a dictatorship, it would be impossible to voice resistance.

Different interpretations of freedom and responsibility clash. On the one hand, there is the freedom to be vaccinated or not, to wear a mask or not, to follow government instructions or not. This comes along with questioning overarching rules and regulations, as well as government and other public institutions, and the freedom to recognize them or not. On the other hand, there is a great sense of responsibility of the government to protect its citizens against illness and disease. This responsibility is transferred to citizens as well, who are expected to follow government regulations as their civic duty. COVID-19 has created two distinct realities in which people navigate, both with the absolute claim of being right.

The political scientist and journalist, Anne Applebaum, highlights that polarization is not just a problem between political parties but also among the liberal left. She has studied Poland and Hungary and finds that it is diffuse feelings that promote an anti-liberal thinking. Those feelings are provoked by a fear of relegation, of losing political autonomy, or by the adaption of national heroism. Interestingly, Anne Applebaum discovered that the people with anti-liberal sentiments are not those who are likely to be exposed to the related risks; it is not those whose jobs are threatened by immigrants, and it is not the provincial "somewheres" who protest against the supremacy of the cosmopolitan "anywheres." Anti-liberal thinking is made possible by the representatives of the intellectual and conservative elites who actively support illiberal statesmen seeking to change the rules of democracy. They represent a conservative elite, and this elite acts out of a feeling of somehow having come out short. They are afraid that they may not be able to hold their social status in the long run. They feel individually entitled to their status and they are afraid that a societal readjustment of wealth may leave them empty handed. Anne Applebaum suggests that a part of the challenge may lie in the difference and often even the contradiction of the expectations of an individual citizen and the rights of a community.[1] The issue of individual freedom and civic duty has certainly broadened societal polarization.

Friedrich Nietzsche defined civil duty as "the right others have of us." Recognizing the rights of others in the pursuit of one's own rights may have gone out of fashion. The German philosopher, Richard David Precht, suggests that assuming the rights of others is part of an attitude one assumes – an attitude toward others and toward institutions and, most importantly, an attitude toward oneself.[2]

Older generations may recall the imposition to wear a seat belt or not to smoke in public. These social requirements have become the norm and resistance to them lays dormant in distant memory. Nowadays, those defying social impositions have been led into the muddy waters of fundamental, alternative interpretations. The COVID-19 crisis has helped un-dig the age-old narrative of victim and perpetrator, suggesting there are different realities that exist – different views of right and wrong.

We often forget that the real question is not if the state can or cannot impose duties, but which kinds of duties and for what reason. Modern democracy not only has the right to impose regulations and measures for the protection of millions of exposed and vulnerable citizens, it has a duty to do so. In the development of the nation state, the emergence of the civic state occurred across most of Western Europe in the 19th century. Civic states emerged in revolutions from the domination of the few over the many that dictated the previous centuries. Civic states embraced the notion of increasing the well-being of all of its citizens, backed by human rights. The right to be protected from the state has been replaced by the right to be protected by the state.

At the time, Wilhelm von Humboldt and John Stuart Mill had helped shape a new understanding of freedom: The freedom of the individual stops where it limits the fundamental freedom of others. Being protected by society has become as much a civil right as individual self-expression. Since the 19th century, public hygiene has become an increasingly important state duty – and this is where COVID-19 comes in. The modern state has a duty to protect its weaker citizens and ensuring the well-being for all by imposing regulations. The question to consider is about the proportionality of the imposed regulations. To prevent a moral dictatorship, proportionality needs to be discussed and agreed upon.

Richard David Precht suggests that the two guard rails in the discussion are the fundamental rights of the individual, on the one side, and the collective responsibility for the well-being of all, on the other side. The space between these guard rails needs to be navigated in a transparent and adaptive process. To achieve such transparency and adaptability, those participating in the discussion need to understand and embrace the underlying human connection between all citizens. They need to share a sense of all of us being in this together. Building bridges to enable listening to others is a critical part of creating a space for a real conversation and dialogue.

Needing to overcome polarized conflicts

While a certain degree of polarization is healthy for democracy, history shows that extreme polarization can destroy it. The collapse of the German and Spanish democracies in the 1930s, then Chile in 1973, and more recently Thailand, Turkey, and Venezuela in the early 2000s serve as historic examples. In each case, competing parties have considered each other as an existential threat to the extent that they rather undermined the democracy than accept a victory of the opposing side.

In the 1960s, only 4% of the Democrats and 5% of the Republicans in the United States had an issue if their child married a person from the other party. Fifty years later, in 2010, the feelings have changed radically. Now, 33% of Democrats and 49% of Republications would not be pleased to have a daughter or son in law from the opposing party.[3] In the past decade, things have deteriorated further. About 60% of both parties say they believe that the other party is a "serious threat for the United States."[4] The degree of hatred between the two parties is unparalleled in the past 100 years of the country's history.

Badly fractured democracies become badly fractured societies. Sooner or later, political opponents become enemies and anybody who speaks differently is considered a traitor. The difficult handover of power from the Trump to the Biden administration, along with the attack on the U.S. capital in early 2021, bear witness to the deterioration of a society that has lost its acceptance of democratic rules. While this extreme violence as a result of a strong polarization may be particularly strong in countries with a strong dual-party system, Europe has experienced more violence at the edges of more frequent demonstrations, too. The journey from a polarized sense of violence to the ability to sit at the same table and constructively discuss and resolve a shared issue is long and thorny. Nonetheless, we must find a way forward to save our societies.

In the past two decades across Europe, new models of citizen involvement in finding political solutions have been explored. Traditionally, citizen engagement was limited to voting, demonstrations, and petitions. Nowadays, given the acceptance of an online environment, citizen engagement has broadened in many nations to include referendums, public consultations, and a participation in political deliberation. These new means of engagement are broadly called deliberate participatory instruments. The deliberate participatory instruments are being tested to measure to what degree the decision-making process can be advanced by hearing objections and including a broader perspective ahead of a finalized political solution.

The context of our sustainability challenges has further broadened the inclusion of stakeholders. The type of measures we need to address the sustainability challenges of these times requires government to work with business in a new manner, too. Pioneers in business have become active in seeking a seat at the table to push future-oriented legislation. The Commission of the European Union has been particularly successful in engaging in dialogues with a broad stakeholder base and as a result launching far-reaching highly disruptive new legislation in the area of data privacy and security as well as circular economy and sustainability. For example, the production of single-use plastic has been prohibited with an ambitious time schedule and business has proven very able to develop and scale alternative solutions.

If you would like to implement a project that requires the contribution of a wider group of stakeholders, you likely end up in a challenging situation. Projects that address a societal or environmental issue require bringing together people with different opinions about both the problem and the solution. Importantly, a first step is needed before a conflict can be explored and resolved. People need to be convinced to even be in the same room. The issue is no longer just of a transactional nature whereby the parties involved all benefit from a common interest solution. Polarization now demands a mindset transformation acknowledging that a solution must benefit a greater good beyond the two parties. Such a greater benefit is required so that both realities can fit into the same room. Consequently, bringing stakeholders across sectors into the same room – virtual or real – has become a considerable first challenge. Only a truly gifted facilitator can create and hold a space such that everybody feels heard and respected. This is a required starting base for envisioning collaboration.

This book explores what it takes to achieve such collaboration, studying the mindset transformation required for an individual and also for a group or an organization. We explore alternatives and options to deal with such an explosive situation. We investigate different options for changing minds, both our own and those of others. Furthermore, we discover that simply sitting down with an open mind and an open heart requires much pre-work and a few important pre-conditions.

Notes

1 Ribi, T. (2021): Warum sind Autokraten so attraktiv? *NZZ Feuilleton*, March 30, accessed online July 5, 2021: www.nzz.ch/feuilleton/was-macht-autokraten-attraktiv-anne-applebaum-sucht-antworten-id.1608885
2 Precht, R.D. (2021): *Von der Pflicht. Eine Betrachtung*. Munich: Wilhelm Goldmann Verlag.
3 Ziblatt, D., and Levitsky, S. (2021): The despair of the old majority: American Conservatives risk the democracy. *Wissenschaftszentrum Berlin für Sozialforschung (WZB) Mitteilungen*, (17), 6–9.
4 Kalmoe, N.P., and Mason, L. (2019): Lethal mass partisanship: Prevalence, correlates, and electroal contingencies. Contribution to the NCAPSA American Politics Meeting. Washington, DC, 2019, accessed online May 4, 2021: www.dannyhayes.org/uploads/6/9/8/5/69858539/kalmoe___mason_ncapsa_2019_-_lethal_partisanship_-_final_lmedit.pdf

4 Embracing a new level of complexity

Short story: Anja's journey back from conspiracy theories

Anja Sanchez Mengeler is in her mid-40s and lives in the north of Germany. She had been a citizen with an open, liberal mindset, until personal frustration and suggestive articles of internet friends had turned her to embrace a conspiracy-based worldview. Ingrid Brodnig has documented Anja's interesting case of how to let go of a conspiracy-based worldview and return to her previous liberal and open mindset. Anja's journey back from the alternative reality was long, taking a couple of years. She says the one thing that truly facilitated her journey back was the persistence of her sister and her husband who refused to give up on her. They found manners to connect to her by creating mini-moments highlighting small common grounds. Her sister would share cooking recipes and share daily trivia about her kids. Her husband found ways to talk about anything but the sensitive issues they disagreed on, and specialized in creating small, positive moments of sharing and enjoyment. They both knew that letting Anja go was no option and Anja perceived this as the unconditional support she needed. For her, it eventually proved essential to slowly change her mind without losing face.[1]

Creating a space for Anja to change had nothing to do with convincing her to change; it was all about creating shared spaces of humanness and connection that gave her a potential future to step into and to trust in. Changing her mind was enabled by a patient, loving field that was purposefully larger than the space of disagreement. Finding your voice in this polarized world may have little to do with improving your argumentative ability; it may be all about your capacity to be there for somebody you care about and who currently strongly disagrees with you. Anja's story shows that it is about enlarging the shared world to

DOI:10.4324/9781003305941-5

include items and moments of shared appreciation, positivity, and care. Those moments remove the all-consuming topics of disagreement.

This short story demonstrates the power of the human connection as a means to build a broader foundation and a bridge for a person who lives in a different reality to reconnect back to a reality that they have lost. It takes incredible courage to do so, and I believe that the strength provided by the human connection is an important source for the required courage.

Working together in a polarized world

Communication strategies offer a different access to overcoming both classic and polarized conflicts. Julie Schumacher Cohen, assistant vice president of community engagement and government affairs at the University of Scranton, United States, suggests that any communication is basically a translation exercise. Whenever we communicate, we translate what happens in our own world for others living in their world who may hold different worldviews. The more aware we are of the context of our communication, the better we can contextualize what we say such that it can be heard.[2]

Shamil Idriss, CEO of Search for Common Ground, a global NGO focused on ending violent conflict, has studied what actually transforms people. It is almost never the experience of being shouted down or shut out that brings about change. It is the "human connection with the very people that you have learned to hate that will transform you."[3] Particularly, when different worldviews are in play, the human connection is a critical first step. Shamil Idriss also points out the difference between debates and dialogue. Debates are places where opponents present their views without acknowledging the other; dialogues are spaces where participants have an uninterrupted space to express themselves. Creating spaces for human connections is part of the solution for building bridges and for working together in a polarized world.

A dialogue with a political opponent requires listening and mutual respect that can be developed through a human connection. Yet, the willingness to create such a connection has disappeared on both sides. Russell Ronald Reno, editor of a publication at First Things, an educational institute that aims to advance religiously informed public philosophy, frames this thinking as follows: "Our moment calls for witness, not dialogue."[4] This observation is reflected in the refusal of young journalists to report neutrally. The emergence of alternative realities has caused a sentiment of having to point out and stand by the truth. Many consider dialogue as risking an unprincipled compromise or a watering-down of such truth. Suggesting dialogue in such a context is anything but evident.

As Anja's story demonstrated earlier, there are other options. In family settings and with friends, you can avoid the divisive topic and create a positive space for friendship, love, and support. This is a realistic and powerful alternative to enable somebody who has succumbed to conspiracy theories a path back to their previous worldview.

Resolving any kind of conflict demands a curiosity to understand what lies underneath the surface, what the other side most fears losing. When faced with polarized conflict, the search for common ground and shared values as a foundation to build a shared vision becomes critical. As we have observed, to reach that stage, a space for human connection needs to be created – and in that space we can engage in dialogue with those we disagree with.

When we need to work with people who hold distinctly different positions or opinions, we face a more pragmatic situation. This refers, for example, to people with whom we feel no particular bond but who are mission-critical to the success of a project we seek to implement. What does it take to create a space both within us as well as for us and the other person such that we can find a common ground of collaboration? We have explored several options and have also learned that attempting to convince the other with facts or by exposing them to shortcomings in their thinking will only harden their position.

What works is to create a human connection so that both sides – us and them – can see the individual, the human being, rather than just the conflicting position in the other. This is particularly important when a polarized conflict needs to be overcome. How do we acquire this ability, and what is needed for the other person to join in this adventure? The challenge is clear and the urgency is pressing.

Comparing classic with polarized conflict

We have thus far focused on exploring how the challenge of working together has become so much more complicated since polarization has become a phenomenon that concerns society at large.

Classic conflicts are typically based on disagreements and tensions that occur in a shared reality. This means that the persons involved in the conflicts hold the same or a very similar worldview while disagreeing mildly to violently how to live and operate in that reality. Human beings have been exposed to such classic conflicts at the personal, the organizational, and the societal levels and there are well-proven conflict management and mediation approaches that work well in such cases. Such conflicts include conflicts of interest that occur between employers and employees or between different parties negotiating a deal. My book entitled "Five Superpowers for Co-creators" falls into this category. It offers a simple but effective trick in multistakeholder collaboration, suggesting tensions and disagreements be viewed as overstretched opposing strengths. When uncovering the two strengths involved, it becomes possible to recognize the value in both and embracing the meta-level of identifying the superpower that combines both strengths. Such approaches only work when the parties involved are able to actually listen to each other with an open heart and mind – something that works in classic conflicts but not in polarized conflicts.

As we have discovered in Part I of this book, when a polarized conflict exists, the initial step consists of connecting opposing parties together so that they can listen to each other. This initial step is not required in a classic conflict, where opposing parties can typically agree to explore options to solve their issue (see Figure 4.1).

Integral theory is of help in understanding this step zero. Don Beck and Christopher Cowan explain different worldviews from a human evolution perspective as different levels of consciousness.[5] While they carefully point out that there is value judgment associated with different levels of consciousness, Beck and Cowan highlight that each level builds on the next, and that we are all capable of thinking on each of these levels. For

Figure 4.1 Comparing a classic conflict with a polarized conflict – connect

example, when a person is hungry and desperately looks for something to eat, the person thinks out of an instinctive mindset. On the other hand, when a person actually realizes that it is possible to care about the planet and others while also making a good living, the person thinks out of a systemic mindset. The main aspects to remember is that all levels are important and necessary for human evolution and that there is no better or higher level. We can therefore consider that the two worldviews belong to two very different levels of consciousness, and that bridging them is not possible until we have created a common ground from which to understand that we can indeed perceive things from different perspectives.

As a closing thought for this part of the book, I would like to share the wisdom of the integral theory in the form of three key principles that can help guide us in finding the human connection again.[6] **Humility** suggests that it is wise to accept that all perspectives are true. Consequently, humility also suggests that in this sense, everyone is right. Integral theory suggests that we can practice noticing when we assume or judge that someone's perspective is wrong, and that we can practice extending our perspective and become more inclusive. **Discernment** is an important additional principle that says all perspectives are false. This is to say that while we may be capable of including another's perspective, we also stand by our own perspective and truth with dignity and self-respect not to collapse into someone else's worldview. **Enactment** points to our responsibility to express our values and to shepherd ever more integral conversations. How can this be achieved? By applying humility and discernment in all conversations we engage in.

Notes

1 Brodnig, I. (2021): *Einspruch! Verschwörungsmythen und Fake News kontern – in der Familie, im Freudeskreis und online*. Wien: Brandstätter.
2 Young, J. (2020). The art of communication in a polarized world. *Journal of Cultural Analysis and Social Change*, 5(2), 16: https://doi.org/10.20897/jcasc/9326
3 Schumacher Cohen, J. (2019): Polarized word dialogue – radical act. *American Magazine*, December 3: www.americamagazine.org/politics-society/2019/12/03/polarized-world-dialogue-radical-act
4 Ibid.
5 Beck, D.E., and Cowan, C.C. (2005): *Spiral Dynamics: Mastering Values, Leadership and Change*. Chichester: John Wiley and Sons Ltd.
6 Segatori,S.(2017):Whatisintegralphilosophy,integraltheory?Extractfromthe "Integral Center Membership Manual" in Boulder Colorado: https://medium.com/@ssegatori/what-is-integral-philosophy-integral-theory-5c6b0ccc7724

Part II

From transaction to transformation

Part II seeks inspiration from stories and cases where a collaboration was possible despite significant differences of opinions. Different stories explore what works best in classic and polarized situations and provide insights on how to keep working together in a polarized world.

For example, in his role as CEO of Unilever, Paul Polman discovered the power of creating a pre-competitive space in which competitors could together resolve societal issues any one of them would not consider addressing alone. This has inspired his current activity at the Imagine Foundation where he pro-actively hosts such pre-competitive talks across sectors around the world.

The in-depth case study highlights a successful cross-sector multistakeholder initiative in Switzerland called PRISMA. The project analysis draws out important lessons learned in how to create a system change required to trigger a cross-sector innovation. The case study offers insights not only into both a classic and a polarized conflict but also into how to overcome both classic conflicts that occurred at the beginning of the project and polarized conflicts once the recommendations were to be implemented. The project also showcases the role of business in pro-actively shaping new regulation that serves society and the planet. Lastly, the multiyear journey provides concrete proof that conflicts can be overcome and shines a first light on the underlying mindset requirements of a successful multistakeholder collaboration.

We refer to research insights that clarify these underlying mindsets both at a leadership and an organizational level. A comparison of the different mindset highlights the need for a positive impact mindset and sheds a first light on the extent of the challenge of a mindset transformation.

DOI:10.4324/9781003305941-6

The story of a Swiss city attempting to integrate the Sustainable Development Goals (SDGs) into the city's strategy highlights the challenges, near failures, and ultimate success factors of such complex projects. The story highlights the importance of finding approaches to keep a dialogue going when disagreement and division pulls opposing parties apart. It becomes obvious how important it is to find a shared higher purpose that all involved parties can step up to beyond their own realities. Stepping up to embrace such a shared purpose is the key to the transformation needed to overcome polarization and outlines the realm beyond the transactional mindset of classic conflicts.

5 Finding a shared purpose

Short story: the pre-competitive space

Paul Polman, former CEO of Unilever, describes an interesting encounter among CEOs of competing ice-cream brands. When he became CEO of Unilever, he was on the lookout for opportunities to reduce the organization's negative impact on the climate. When examining the CO_2 footprint of their ice-cream operation across the value chain, they identified the importance of the greenhouse gas emissions of the chlorofluorocarbon (CFC) and hydrofluorocarbon (HFC) engines in the refrigerators, which store the ice cream at points of sale. As different ice cream brands were kept in these refrigerators, no single ice cream producer could address this issue and none of them had ever thought about engaging their competitors in a conversation not only about the climate impact of these refrigerators but also, more importantly, about alternative planet-friendly solutions. These refrigerators contribute to about 3% of the annual global warming. Paul managed to convince the CEOs of the top four global ice-cream producers to meet in one room, and the four of them decided to invest in developing a natural refrigerant replacing the existing engines. This required persuading various governments involved to approve new regulation to override the very strong lobby of CFC and HFC producers. Ultimately, the CEOs succeeded in creating a CO_2-emission-free engine that was both cheaper and used less energy, benefitting all points of sales with these fridges. Owing to Paul's out-of-the-box thinking and the collaboration of these CEOs, they identified and implemented a solution to reduce a significant contributor to climate change.

Paul Polman calls such discussions "creating a pre-competitive space." This refers to a space where competitors can meet and jointly discuss issues, which no single player alone could address and resolve. Just imagine what kinds of challenges could be

DOI:10.4324/9781003305941-7

resolved in this manner. Paul states boldly and clearly that there is "no competition about our future."[1] His work at the Foundation Imagine is about creating such pre-competitive spaces, hosting similar conversations across industries and markets. He is adamant about including as much of the supply chain as is required to solve a problem.

What might the characteristics of a pre-competitive space in politics be? Could we also pretend that there is no competition about the future in politics? Is there such a thing? Are there politicians who are willing to meet and jointly address issues that need solving without delivering them or their party an immediate or direct benefit, such as these four CEOs did?

The social and environmental challenges of our time would benefit greatly from such shared issues. Clearly, different stakeholders are needed to craft future-relevant solutions and these include also new and more appropriate regulations to incite the positive change while penalizing economic behavior that continues harming the planet and society. Many of these issues could be at least partially resolved through such pre-competitive spaces. Social labs as explored by various practitioners including Otto Scharmer with his U labs, can be considered as such pre-competitive spaces. They are often even broader in terms of problem definition and include a large variety of smaller players that bring in new, fresh ideas.

Pre-competitive spaces can be of relevance when we create spaces for multistakeholder sessions that include participants of different backgrounds, interests, and ideologies. Such spaces are very much based on the creation of a human connection. Indeed, nobody would show up if it was not for the interest in establishing such a deeper connection. The human connection creates an energy in the room that allows considering new perspectives of a higher ground and a shared vision that serve more than just the individual players involved.

Multistakeholder co-creation as a lever for change

My experience with such pre-competitive spaces derives from a concept we call the Collaboratory. The Collaboratory was inspired by the challenge of how to transform business schools to become relevant breeding places for responsible and sustainable leaders. It was piloted at the RIO+20 United Nations Conference in Rio de Janeiro in June 2012. Thereafter, many attendees started to explore its usefulness in various settings including business, education, social conflict, and multistakeholder debates. The book entitled "The Collaboratory"[2] bears testimony of the many applications and explains the underlying conceptual foundations including Theory U, circle practice, dialogue forms, and various inspirations from existing social labs from around the world.

The Collaboratory allowed us to build the prototypes for the EU research project Leadership for Transition (LiFT), where we tested one-day Collaboratory events across Europe between 2014 and 2018.[3] The events taught us how to create and hold spaces where stakeholders with opposing views felt comfortable to share their views. The trust created early on in the day enabled participants to start listening to perspectives that were foreign to them. We identified many factors that enabled this trusting space, such as the physical appearance of the room with chairs staged in circles so that everybody could see everybody. The Collaboratory also included the feature of a talking stick (or speaking stone), which opposes a debate. Furthermore, the clear design of opening statements that presented the different perspectives without debating them enabled what Otto Scharmer calls a downloading. Everybody present offloaded what was on their minds and slowly emptied it out so that hearing the other and becoming open to new ideas could take place. Setting up such clear ground rules builds trust that there is a facilitator in charge with no share in the outcome, focusing on the process of ensuring that everybody is respected while also providing an opportunity for the quieter voices in the room to be heard and considered. The book entitled "The Collaboratory" describes these and other factors.[4]

These prototypes generated important insights into how to address and overcome classic conflicts of such multistakeholder events. These challenges arise for individual participants, for groups across participating organizations, and for the facilitators holding the space. The successor book entitled "Five Superpowers for Co-creators"[5] is a comprehensive user manual leading through these classic conflict challenges and offers step-by-step building blocks for creating innovation journeys for new solutions.

Nowadays, I spend half of my consulting time helping forward-thinking actors in an industry or a sector to figure out how to jointly identify solutions to a societal challenge that has become pressing for them. What I had to learn in recent years is that conflicts have become more complex than in the past. It may well be that today the co-creation journey includes not just classic conflicts but also more complex polarized conflicts. Coming up with a vision is one thing; translating that vision into concrete implementation pathways is another. As new visions are introduced into an existing context, there can suddenly be two conflicting realities at hand – and these realities may represent a polarized conflict. In the PRISMA case it is evident that the existing consumer waste-collection reality operates from a very different logic than the new vision, and existing players often have more to lose than to win when they consider the new vision. This creates a strong tension.

Finding approaches to make it attractive for existing players to embrace new solutions often requires facilitation to be more similar to conflict mediation. It is helpful to understand what type of conflict needs to be resolved. In case of a polarized conflict, the facilitator will need to enable the opposing parties to see and hear each other before applying proven methods that work for classic conflicts. Seeing and hearing the other starts with stepping down from the polarized position and finding a way to recognize that the person in front is a human being. This human connection is the major initial step to downgrade polarized conflicts into the sphere of classic conflicts. In the next section, we consider a further difference between classic and polarized conflicts.

From transactional to transformational

One may think that once a facilitator has managed to create a human connection between parties of a polarized conflict, the remaining steps can be approached like in a classic conflict. Here is what we have learned: these conflicts are different in nature. While a classic conflict can be overcome using conflict resolution approaches that are based in a transactional logic, polarized conflicts require a transformational approach. In a transactional logic, win-win solutions work well. All that is needed is that both parties have something to gain that they value, and usually a solution can be found. In a polarized issue, once the parties sit at the table and are able to see and hear each other, they need to rise up to sharing a higher vision that typically benefits more than just the parties involved. Instead of just realizing the shared interest of finding a solution that is of mutual benefit, in this instance the parties need to agree to a higher-level truth – and that requires a transformational approach.

Let us consider a real-life case of such a multistakeholder innovation process across a sector. I reflect on the success of such projects with Simone Alabor. She is the initiator of the project known as PRISMA Innovation, a cross-sector project to reinvent consumer waste in the context of the burgeoning plastic waste problem in Switzerland, which we explore in full depth in the next chapter.

There are a number of pre-conditions for cross-sector, multistakeholder co-creation initiatives to succeed. To Simone, it is clear that such initiatives must start in the market. Cross-sector projects need the economy on their side so that the needed regulatory changes can eventually be made to enable a new and better solution.

We identified two critical moments for such initiatives:

1. The time of the launch of the project.
2. The moment the project is exposed to the current system and existing players.

First, when choosing the moment to launch a new initiative, there must be significant pressure in the industry in which a new initiative is launched. Such pressure may occur due to a rise in consumer concern or there may be new legislation on the national or international horizon that will impact the current market model. Furthermore, there needs to be an obvious innovation gap caused by existing players' refusal to change. This occurs in industries protected by powerful lobbyists that are able to artificially protect an industry or market from changes that are visible on the horizon. To launch a project, it is imperative to have a few highly motivated individuals in key positions of relevant organizations, who are interested in working together and are able to dedicate time and resources to such an initiative over a prolonged period. These people are innovators and pioneers, true change agents both within and often beyond and across their current careers. In that first moment, there is no obvious conflict to resolve, as the parties that will join such a project all agree on the need to change, even if the solution may not yet be clear.

Second, when the project is ready to go public, it is pertinent to ensure that the initiative has a clear vision of the purported new world to be realized. A new world here means a solid understanding of the final ideal vision to be accomplished. This vision is likely to be in stark contrast with the current world. This is where a polarized conflict may emerge. When exposing such an initiative to existing players, this vision needs to be as clear and solid as possible to face the likely strong reactions against it. It is as if different worldviews confront each other. Simone Alabor calls it a framework – a blueprint – that operationalizes the new state of the industry. Such a framework helps illustrate the ideal vision in a more concrete manner and is critical to ensure a certain amount of credibility when discussing a new vision. Furthermore, the framework also helps ensure that the new vision does not collapse when being exposed to the current worldview. Introducing a new vision to an existing market reality is likely to result in high tensions and battles and may well require new legislation to force a change in the reality. In the next section, let us consider the real case of the PRISMA initiative in Switzerland.

Notes

1 Polman, P. (2021): Infliction points for senior leaders. Video interview in Wendepunkt by Dennis Shuler: www.kineticconsulting.com/2021/02/wendepunkt-inflection-points-for-senior-leaders-with-paul-polman/
2 Muff, K. (ed.) (2014): *The Collaboratory – A Co-creative Stakeholder Engagement Process for Solving Complex Problems*. Sheffield: Greenleaf Publishing.
3 Leadership for Transition, a EU-funded multi-phase research project: http://leadership-for-transition.eu/?page_id=36
4 Muff, K. (ed.) (2014): *The Collaboratory – A Co-creative Stakeholder Engagement Process for Solving Complex Problems*. Sheffield: Greenleaf Publishing.
5 Muff, K. (2019). *Five Superpowers for Co-creators – How Change Makers and Business Can Achieve the Sustainable Development Goals*. Sheffield: Routledge.

6 A practice case – trans-sectoral stakeholder collaboration

Case study: PRISMA – a business-led multistakeholder project

Switzerland faces an interesting challenge with regard to its current household and consumer product waste. While Switzerland is considered good at recycling, not all materials are indeed collected for recycling. Particularly, the growing amount and diversity of plastic waste is of major concern. Furthermore, food and beverage producers are keen to have access to the recycled raw materials such that they can package their goods in recyclable and ideally also in recycled packaging. The producer initiative PRISMA (www.PRISMA-Innovation.ch) was launched to resolve the existing and increasingly outdated household waste collection system in Switzerland. In the past, a high rate of recyclability was the definition of success in consumer waste treatment; in the day and age of circular economy thinking, recycling and incineration are the last resort.

The current household waste system in Switzerland is organized by material fraction. Paper and cartons, PET bottles, tin plate and aluminum cans, glass containers, and, increasingly, the wet organic food waste are collected from homes by separate independent organizations. All waste that is not collected through such an independent organization belongs lawfully to the cantons, which usually delegates this responsibility to their municipalities. Such waste is often used as fuel for district heating solutions. The material fractions are collected by separate national organizations, which have formed a Swiss Recycling Association as their common communication and lobbying platform. The huge increase in different types of plastic waste in the past years causes a serious challenge to the system. It is unclear who should be in charge of collecting, separating,

DOI:10.4324/9781003305941-8

and recycling the different types of plastic waste. Should there be new material fractions? Or should the retailer collect the growing range of plastic at the point of sale? And what about the increasing waste generated in the public space with the huge increase in food and drinks consumed on the go? While Swiss regulations are slow, the European Commission has announced a number of directives ranging from a ban of certain single-use plastic items to legislation that demands all plastic to be recyclable. There is growing consumer pressure too. Sensitized to the problem of plastic waste pollution in our oceans, consumers expect food producers to package their goods in either recyclable or recycled materials. The producers' current demand for granular plastic to produce recycled packaging items by far outpaces the supply of such raw material.

Food and food packaging producers, often operating across Europe and needing to comply with the stricter European norms, are highly interested in finding solutions that work universally. A few important pioneers launched the PRISMA Initiative in 2018. By 2021, PRISMA was in intense negotiations with the existing umbrella organization of the various independent Swiss recyclers. These discussions are made of the same stuff as polarized conflicts. There are indeed two different realities facing one another: the current system and the ideal future vision. The representatives of the current system fear that they will lose out. The PRISMA pioneers wanted a solution for a current problem. The two worlds could not be more different.

Once it became clear that the new vision would not go away, the representatives of the existing system decided to embrace the situation and to lead a process that would expand the capacity of the current reality. This decision was the attempt of existing players to actively shape their future. Representatives of PRISMA are a part of that project and propose a more current governance system that seeks to balance the decision-making power among current and future players. In parallel, the threat of a legislative solution continues as an important driver for the project. It ensures that the pressure remains high for all involved players to find a workable solution. The threat of a legislative solution contains a transformative element: Either the current system reinvents itself or a new legislation will dictate the terms of the reinvention.

Case analysis

This case study offers insight into a multistakeholder process that involves business across a sector as well as government. It highlights key enabling conditions that make such a process possible. The case study also shows how an apparently smooth process of envisioning a new, better approach to a societal issue – consumer waste management – can become complex.

The PRISMA vision served as a counterweight to a strong existing market reality. PRISMA members consisted of people with a sense of unity that brought an important counterweight to this polarized situation. Simone Alabor was at the heart of the initial core group that had PRISMA launched. When they selected the initial group of pioneers, they searched for the right kinds of individuals rather than representatives of important organizations. These individuals needed to have an interest for a strategic vision rather than a particular party interest. Instead of experts who would build solutions based on the status quo, PRISMA invited people who knew the context or industry, and who had an ability to observe it rather than be in it. The initial core group understood that it was important that the participants of the initiative would pay a significant annual fee, which would finance the innovation process. An organization that would dedicate a large amount of money would need to have a certain strategic interest in the project.

Once the initial vision was clear, the core group of participants focused on strengthening the core team with big corporate players, as these represented important levers of change. Continuously introducing new participating members to the initiative came with the particular challenge of having to bring such new players along to embrace the previously established vision and work. This approach was followed to avoid having to start all over with every new member joining and required a certain skill when facilitating the innovation session. As their facilitator, I had experience in this challenge.[1] Simone Alabor helped summarize the key challenges we had to address. These key challenges included the following: the strength not to compromise the larger vision, the ability to deal with and live with frustration, and the ability to deal with those who are unable to see the bigger picture and to let them progress in their own time while soliciting support from top management of the various key organizations that we had to onboard. There is a significant difference in culture between an emerging new structure fueled by pioneers compared to a well-established structure representing the current system. PRISMA operated innovatively and democratically, while the existing system operated with an internal decision-making process that was highly traditional, hierarchical, and protective. Simone Alabor pointed out that it is important to know where your red lines are and also to know where and when to budge. To her, that which will win is that which works along the market rules of efficiency. Ultimately, the better concept will win.

Initiatives such as PRISMA work well in a market where cooperation has not worked. PRISMA has provided such a strong alternative to an existing unwavering reality that the current players are being forced to recognize that there is an alternative reality even if they do not like it. Once the new system was ready to be implemented, representatives of the existing system blocked any further progress. The parties involved found themselves in the midst of a polarized conflict. This was visible in the emerging power play of the existing players and the growing new market forces. For the existing players, there was so much at stake. Their ongoing lobbying efforts resulted in a lock-in effect that would hamper any progress. And yet, the new reality was critical to shift the existing system and thinking. A polarization was essential to create a tipping point – and this is where learning to work through polarized conflicts becomes relevant for multistakeholder processes that address societal issues.

Polarization is not all bad; it may be needed to stretch a current reality to such an extent that its worldview cracks and maybe crumbles. What is important is to find means to bridge the two opposing realities to create not only a dialogue but indeed a common agreement that a new, better solution is necessary. For PRISMA, this meant also learning to let go, to a necessary degree, of its ideal vision and to work along with the existing players on a transition solution that would bridge the two worlds. A nearly year-long process among the top representatives of both systems ensured that it was possible to create a human connection between them and that a conversation was possible. Anybody could at any time pick up the phone and talk to the other side.

Case learnings

What we can learn from the PRISMA Collaboratory is that there are means one can apply pressure to the system in the right places and at the right time to create change. We have studied the pre-conditions in Chapter 5. In a polarized world where it is hardly possible to talk with people who hold different opinions, it is refreshing to witness how an innovative co-creation process can contribute to a change of thinking in a previously inflexible system. It is about creating a counterbalance by assembling an important pool of influence and power. Yet, as the case also illustrates, creating an ideal vision among pioneers does not mean the vision can easily be implemented in an existing reality. This is where the challenge of overcoming polarized conflict emerges.

I asked Simone Alabor, the initiator, to reflect on what is required of an initiator to lead such a project. The amazing thing about her was her unwavering energy and drive to disrupt an unhealthy power structure in favor of better, more sustainable, and just solutions. She suggested that a potential initiator of a cross-sector project should have a future-oriented stance and be very committed to the cause so as not to waver from the original vision when conflicts arise. A core competency of such an initiator includes the capacity to be both open and flexible in her or his thinking. This is of central importance when having to integrate new ideas in an ongoing process of an emergent solution. Such a competency requires a high degree of resilience and a capacity to overcome classic conflicts with ease. This includes outstanding communication skills. In situations of conflict, it also requires the talent to talk with different people who have very different perspectives. Simone Alabor suggested that the intellectual capacity to switch from a macro-level to a micro-level and to know how the other person viewed the system is essential. She is someone who is incredibly fast in her thinking, which has helped reframe situations that might otherwise have resulted in conflicts.

Part of the success of creating a powerful vision was the innovation approach we had selected. We used Otto Scharmer's Theory U process that involved co-creating an ideal future. We started with the future and from there figured out how to create solutions in the present. This approach taught us that we needed to operate on two distinctly different levels. The meta-level was about preparing the ground for a revolutionary new industry agreement; the micro-level was about show-casing how innovative solutions in the various critical aspects of waste collection, separation, recycling, production, and sale could indeed solve the many challenges we had to overcome to create that ideal future vision.

Co-creation involved a process of securing consensus among an ever-growing group. We had the chance of having an extraordinary core group. Their ability to critically reflect on objectives and results in the context of a fast-changing market dynamic during innovation sessions brought an amazing degree of authentic urgency to the meetings, which helped draw new members in. There was a real and honest effort to keep figuring out what was most needed irrespective of what had been planned, and that turned these innovation meetings into extremely lively and real high-relevance sessions.

The key challenge for the PRISMA representatives and the representatives of the existing system was in agreeing on a higher shared vision. While they did connect on a human basis, they still used predominantly transactional arguments to try and advance toward a solution. This is when we discovered that polarized conflicts differ in more than one respect from classic conflicts. It will take more than a shared interest to find a solution. It will take an agreement on a solution that lies above and beyond the understanding of both sides. The existing system needs to understand the time has come to embrace a new era, and the PRISMA representatives will need to acknowledge that their ideal vision needs to be adapted to the less ideal reality of existing structures, regulations, and manners of doing business that fall short of what ideally would make most sense. The involved parties are in the process of accomplishing this shift from seeking purely transactional win-win solutions among parties present to a transformational solution. They start envisioning benefits far greater than serving only those parties present, such as creating a circular resource system that will keep all packaging material in the loop instead of being burned. Once this shift is completed, the new Swiss consumer packaging circularity will serve as a truly transformational solution to which all required parties contributed. At the time of writing, not all players are there yet, with those blocking the progress still preferring transactional solutions highlighting the need to bring all critical players to agree on the shared higher vision.

Note

1 Muff, K. (2018): *Five Superpowers for Co-creators*. Routledge: www.5superpowers.org

7 Dedicated to a higher cause

The "we" mindset of leaders

The shift from a transactional to a transformational logic requires a mindset shift. To better understand the enablers of such a shift, we began searching for situations where we could observe such a shift. We started at an obvious place: organizations with leaders who have created visions that not only serve their direct interests but that seek to create value for society and the world. Such visions require a transformative logic that is based on the understanding that we are all just a small part of something much larger and that success is defined as helping the larger system succeed.

In my organizational research, we have called organizations with such an objective "Positive Impact Organizations" (PIOs). The idea of PIOs builds on a framework I had developed with Thomas Dyllick, at the time Professor of Sustainability Management at the University of St. Gallen. The framework differentiates between organizations that perceive sustainability mostly as a risk and those that recognized that sustainability challenges are, in fact, business opportunities.[1] It takes a mindset shift to shift from a risk focus to an opportunity focus. To understand how this shift can be accomplished, we involved a group of doctoral students and together we studied 13 advanced sustainability organizations from 2013 to 2018.[2] Interestingly, this mindset shift can be observed in the leader and the organization.

Our research found that the leader's mindset can be defined by its perspective. The leadership mindset considers the organization from the outside in. It takes into account the world at large, what is happening outside of the organization, and then derives the strategy for the organization from the outside-in perspective. This compares to a traditional inside-out perspective where a leader's focus is firmly set within the organization

DOI:10.4324/9781003305941-9

and considers anything that happens outside of its boundaries as outside of its direct concerns or priorities. I call the inside-out as compared to the outside-in perspective also the "me" versus the "we" mindset. The two perspectives are reflected in how a leader creates value. The traditional leader with a "me" mindset focuses on direct stakeholders that are directly served, shareholders and employees in particular. An outside-in leader with a "we" mindset creates value for both those outside of its boundaries and for those inside of it. They create a positive impact for the planet and for society. These leaders have redefined how they interpret their role and the role of their organization. Such leaders understand their purpose as providing a positive value to society and the environment while being capable to align internal processes to ensure the organization's long-term financial health in this larger purpose.

Looking deeper into this mindset to understand how it differs from traditional leadership approaches, Isabel Rimanoczy's insights are helpful.[3] As a sustainability and leadership scholar, she has spent years researching the sustainability mindset. She has identified the ecological worldview and speaks also of a spiritual intelligence that reflects a oneness with nature and a general mindfulness.

The co-creation mindset of organizations

Our research with these Positive Impact Organizations (PIOs) also highlighted that organizations themselves can have a positive impact mindset. Such organizations have managed to engage very differently with external stakeholders than traditional firms would. Traditionally, stakeholder engagement consists of rather formal meetings an organization sets up with an underlying sense of risk aversion. In the organizations' view, stakeholders are often considered a potential threat that needs to be mitigated.

PIOs take a different approach with regard to external stakeholders and consider them as partners. PIOs treat external stakeholders in the same manner they treat their colleagues across departments internally. Such organizations have experienced that a transparent and frank exchange with external stakeholders can bring many positive advantages. External stakeholders are very broadly defined and include far more actors than suppliers and customers. Anybody with a willingness to be constructive and open is welcome to join co-creative sessions that aim at finding new solutions to solve societal issues. PIOs know that only together, and in new constellations, new solutions can emerge. PIOs are capable to work as easily outside of their business boundaries as they work internally across departments.

Isabel Rimanoczy offers several further insights into the organizational mindset. She highlights the importance of systems thinking and points to the importance of a developed emotional intelligence among employees of an organization. This is mirrored in the organization's ability to reflect and can be found in a high degree of self-awareness of teams with a clear sense of purpose among employees. Isabel Rimanoczy calls these ingredients the foundation of creative innovation. I call organizations with this positive impact mindset co-creative organizations.

The mindset transformation

The "we" mindset and the co-creation mindset highlight the transformation challenge at the individual and the organizational level. Earlier, we considered the idea of a pre-competitive space where the ability to comprehend the larger common good is an essential prerequisite for overcoming the polarization challenge.

A positive impact mindset operates very differently from a traditional mindset. Conflicts that occur among those of a traditional mindset can be resolved with transactional approaches. Win-win solutions will work very well, as each party is satisfied when they and their organization walk away having gained something that is important to them. When we are faced with polarized conflicts, we need mindsets that are able to recognize value in solutions that create value and serve a higher purpose. Achieving this takes an outside-in leadership mindset or a co-creative organizational mindset. Both of these mindsets operate from a worldview where they are a part of a larger system instead of a single player in a large system. Their interest lies in protecting and preserving the larger good rather than solely their own concern.

At the individual level, the mindset transformation involves changing from a "me" to a "we" stance. The "me" stance, which could also be called the egoistic view, is all about being closed to the external world. The challenge lies in transforming to a "we" stance. In this stance we feel that we are a part of a larger picture and that we are therefore able and willing to create a personal purpose in life that serves no longer only me but everybody.

At the organizational level, the mindset change is about moving from considering others as competition to recognizing the potential of co-creation with them and the added value this brings. In other words, it is about moving from being focused on the risks that come with collaborating with others to noticing the opportunities.

These are descriptions of pure states – which do not exist in reality. Most of us are able to navigate from one state to the other. Furthermore, describing them as separate serves here to illustrate what is needed from a mindset when we want to resolve conflicts or when we work with others.

Working together with others, be it as an individual or as an organization, can present quite a challenge. Often, what is needed to propel organizations into a space of collaboration is a dire need to find a solution at a systemic level for a problem that cannot be resolved in any different manner.

Notes

1 Dyllick, T., and Muff, K. (2016): Clarifying the meaning of sustainable business – Introducing a typology from business-as-usual to true business sustainability. *Organization & Environment*, 29, 156–174.
2 Muff, K. (2021): Positive impact innovation. *Sustainability*, 13(16), 8891: www.mdpi.com2071-105013168891
3 Rimanoczy, I. (2020): *The Sustainability Mindset Principles – A Guide to Developing a Mindset for a Better World*. London; New York: Routledge.

8 Co-creation resolving societal issues

Short story: a Swiss city brings co-creation to government

A positive impact mindset can be used to solve polarized conflicts, and it is also a great contributor to solving societal and planetary problems. The ability to think in terms of "we" instead of "me," and the capacity to understand that we are all a part of something larger, provides the necessary perspective to tackle problems that one institution alone cannot solve.

Walter Fassbind has been in charge of sustainability in the city of Zug, Switzerland, for a number of years. Passionately creating innovative clean energy solutions and running an organic farm on the side, Walter walks the talk – he is a great example of a positive impact mindset. He is keen on introducing sustainability into the core strategy of the small Swiss city with a reputation for being a highly successful international tax haven. As in any Swiss city, the administration consists of professional experts that manage the various departments, while the city council consists of five politicians who distribute among themselves the roles of department heads. They are appointed to the council every four years and are both bound to their party electoral and also to the requirement to collaborate with the other council members to lead the city in their election period. From Walter's point of view, they ultimately have one common task: to develop the city sustainably. Switzerland runs a multi-party system consisting of a right-wing party, two central parties, and a left-wing party complemented by two green parties, one located on the political left, the other in the political center. Any council at any level of the political system is always a coalition of the elected party members. There is no such thing as an opposition party. This is the Swiss manner of doing democracy; it requires discussion and compromise while at the same time it

DOI:10.4324/9781003305941-10

consists of as much politics as is characteristically observed in nations with a two-party system.

The economic success of the tax haven and crypto valley focus had come at a cost and the population demanded a course correction. The city council assigned Walter the task of realizing this electoral promise. To leverage power, Walter knew that he had to get the professional administration on board. At the next management meeting, he built a sustainability stand that featured a quick survey. "How important is sustainability for the City of Zug?" The answer was clear and resulted in the city council hiring a strategy consultant to help them define a new strategic objective for the city. Walter convinced them that a purely top-down process would not work and he was able to hire his own consultant (me) to develop bottom-up input for the strategy. We chose an interactive innovation process that aimed at highlighting outside-in ideas that thus far had not been considered. The two processes were smartly interconnected and the bottom-up ideas enabled the top-down strategic re-orientation to be reinforced and substantiated with concrete examples. We were fortunate to have had all city council members present in the various innovation sessions we had conducted. Furthermore, while not everybody was equally enchanted by the approach or the ideas, they had been exposed to the passionate voice of the professional administration that was close to the pulse of the city through their daily interaction with their citizens. The purpose of the exercise was to create a long-term strategy for the city with sustainability at the core of the city's priorities while building on the economic foundation that has created the financial stability of the city.

This story is an example of how a multistakeholder process can provide answers on how a city can contribute to outside-in solutions. This is not a story about solving a conflict and there is also an important lesson here. While we have thus far focused on differentiating between different types of conflicts and how to address them, a positive impact mindset is about more than just solving polarized conflicts. The positive mindset with its outside-in focus is perfect for advancing complex situations. The mindset sets up questions and challenges differently, and by focusing on the larger challenge it can help unlock the mindset of more traditional thinkers in the process. Walter points out that the personal interaction with key decision makers was critical in enabling this complex and demanding process. He had previously initiated many small bottom-up projects that were often at the mercy of the political pressures of the moment and had not gained the required importance to bring about the significant re-orientation he believed the city needed. His personal credibility was essential and was an enabler for these all-important personal conversations that he conducted. He is particularly proud of the city council recognizing and appreciating the importance and relevance of the lower-level professional administration in defining the city strategy. He was most pleased that the city council deviated from their initial temptation to simply define a top-down strategy that would be handed down for implementation. Owing to Walter's suggestion, the professional administration's input, including their concrete and inspirational project ideas, were of such profound solidity and built on hands-on experience that the politicians instantly understood the added value of the ideas. The involvement of the professional administration has the long-term advantage of ensuring that those who will implement the strategy are on board with the strategy, as they recognize their ideas and therefore feel ownership of the strategy. The collaboration of the city council and the administration was strengthened through the innovation workshop and has significantly contributed to the appreciation of the council members for their professional staff. Despite important polarization at the council about the importance of a green or social re-focus, this bottom-up and top-down engagement process had resulted in bringing both the right-wing party and the left-wing party on board.

It may well be that Walter's positive impact mindset has not only enabled the creation of interesting ideas for sustainability challenges but has also prevented a potential conflict that may have otherwise emerged among the city council members or among the members of the professional administration. Mindsets are often at play at both the organizational and the individual level, and there are lessons to be learned at both levels.

Keeping the dialogue going

In search of examples, let us shift from the organizational level in the previous story to the individual level. As stated, the different mindsets are at play at both levels. Let us shift back to how a positive impact mindset may help in addressing polarized conflicts. Sometimes, the conflict is of societal nature, sometimes organizational, and at times it is personal. In my experience, individual-level conflicts may challenge us most and may force us out of our comfort zone. For the benefit of exploring solutions, I would like to share a challenging personal situation of my own.

In early summer 2021, my husband and I expected my two godchildren and their parents to visit us for an overnight stay. We looked forward to seeing them and had already prepared the guestrooms and done a bit of the food preparation. It was the time when COVID-19 vaccinations first became available for everybody. While we had not talked about the topic, I had a small hunch that maybe the parents, close friends of us, may not be open to being vaccinated. Since we had planned to also meet with my parents who are high risk given their age and medical situation, I wanted to inquire if my friends were open to do a self-test prior to arrival. Self-tests had just been introduced in Switzerland and every household could pick them up for free at local pharmacies. At that time, the virus was mostly transmitted via children, and this was the first time we would spend an extended indoor time with kids. I texted my girlfriend the morning of arrival, inquiring if they were comfortable to do such self-tests in view of our plans with my parents. I knew instinctively I should have called rather than texted. What happened next was beyond what I had feared. My girlfriend texted back canceling the trip, saying that she and her family did not want to put my parents at risk. She did not explicitly say that she was against self-testing, and consequently we ended up in a bit of a lengthy text message exchange. To her, testing was dangerous and entirely unnecessary in view of a grand manipulation scheme around COVID-19, involving government and the pharma industry. I could not believe that she would put her principles above our friendship. This is how her cancellation landed with me – and she could not believe that I would expect her to test. We had a problem.

I was angry and disappointed – both at her and at myself. I cared much about seeing them all and I realized that I created a friendship crisis. I let a few days pass and then suggested that

I would like to go visit her so that she and I could calmly discuss what had happened and figure out a way forward. Thankfully, she agreed.

A few weeks later, we went for a long walk in the fields of the Swiss Prealps. I started by asking her questions about how she experienced our conversation. The longer I listened, the more I realized that my point of view would be difficult for her to hear. And yet, I also knew that I needed to return the honesty that she offered me. I framed my perspective as carefully as I could, realizing that my judgment of her perspective might cause serious harm to our friendship. I realized in hindsight that she had actually refrained from judging my perspective. In the heat of the moment, I had been too busy sorting out my own thoughts. As our walk continued, we focused on finding common ground, even if this common ground was not found in the topic area. Our points of view were too different. We both reinforced how important our friendship was and, furthermore, how important it was for her kids that we stayed connected and on good terms. This became our shared larger purpose we would focus on. It has become clear that we cannot convince each other on the topic, and yet we also both appreciate that we have a friend on the opposite side that we can talk with to understand the rationale of the other perspective. Having focused on a shared higher purpose was enough to keep our friendship alive.

To me, this personal lived experience enabled me to viscerally know that a mindset is not a stable or acquired state. It changes, depending on the issue and how involved or triggered I am. It also helped me understand that others also do their best and may themselves not be at their best at all times, but what we do is often the best we can do. Taking a step back and understanding from which mindset we act can be very helpful in recalibrating ourselves.

The shared higher vision

In Part II, we have explored examples and cases to learn how to deal with polarized versus classic conflicts. The PRISMA case highlighted that it may take a transformational solution instead of a transactional approach typical for classic differences or conflicts. A transformational solution is always about finding a higher ground, shifting above the perspective of two parties, and to identify a bigger, higher cause to which both can agree. A simple win-win solution will no longer do. When parties can agree on the larger benefit of a shared higher vision, it is possible to proceed. We established this also in the personal account of my individual-level conflict with a friend of mine.

The positive impact mindset that goes along with the capacity to imagine higher purpose visions can be observed both in leaders and organizations. This is what we learned from the Positive Impact Organizations and saw illustrated in the short story about the city of Zug in Switzerland. The importance of a positive impact mindset cannot be underestimated. It is the basic requirement for engaging in any larger societal or environment issue. Such a mindset can sometime change the world.

When Greta Thunberg launched the global youth movement Fridays for Future, the world changed. Until that time, global demonstrations had rarely led to any government reconsidering their choices and priorities. However, 2019 brought about a change and whether they liked it or not, world leaders could no longer ignore the urgent call for action regarding the climate crisis. Ursula van der Leyen included climate change into her election promises to become President of the EU Commission. The EU Commission has taken important measures to combat climate change. The new Green Deal is considered an ambitious political transition project. Regulations around circular economy and plastic waste have forced business and industries across Europe to accelerate their innovation processes. Green parties across Europe achieved significant success in the 2019 elections and had it not been for the COVID-19 pandemic, who knows what might have happened next in the global challenge of fighting climate change.

The positive impact mindset makes it possible to bring about change – be it as an individual or as an organization that embraces the outside-in perspective and chooses to consider sustainability challenges as business opportunities. Often, organizations meet in a pre-competitive space to create together such new market solutions.

What is needed to create such change is a mindset that is very different from a traditional mindset. Leaders and organizations

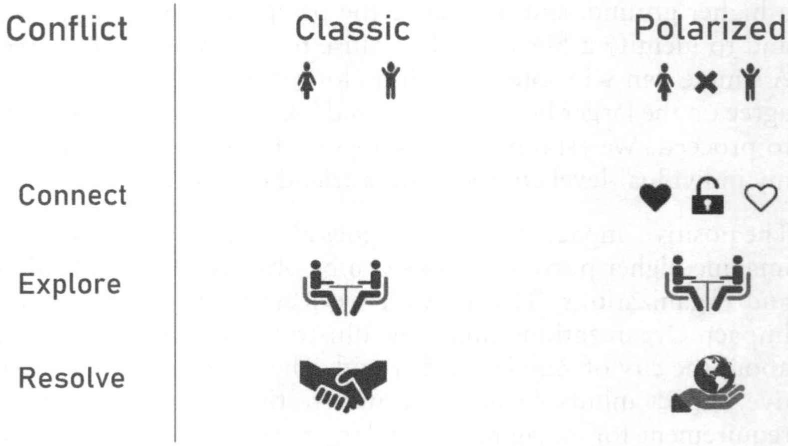

Figure 8.1 Comparing a classic conflict with a polarized conflict – resolve

must be able to experience themselves as part of a larger system they depend on and that they are willing to contribute positively to. Such a mindset requires courage when implementing new types of collaborations with previously unknown actors and it requires the capacity to see beyond one's singular perspective and embrace a shared higher-level truth that is essential to resolve a polarized issue (see Figure 8.1).

Part III

The individual and the organizational challenge

Part III unpacks the challenge for individual leaders and for organizations to transform from a traditional mindset to a positive impact mindset. It explores leading-edge research in this new domain of thinking and highlights the challenge and opportunities with relevant stories and concrete insights. The stories include the successful individual transformation of a Swedish activist leader and the successful organizational transformation of the Swiss World Wildlife Fund (WWF). Furthermore, the stories of a U.S. NGO and of a Swedish city illustrate the benefits of working together across different perspectives and opinions. They highlight the importance of both transformations to enable bridge building in a polarized world.

At the individual level of a leader or change maker, the mindset transformation is about embracing the outside-in perspective that acknowledges as a starting base the existing challenges our society, economy, and the planet faces. This is about a transformation from a "me" to a "we" mindset and it involves a shift from a closed to an open stance in how we consider the world and others. At the organizational level, there is a need to transform from a mindset of competition to one of co-creation. It involves a shift from being risk aware to becoming opportunity aware. Stories from practice and insights from research further explore these two transformations with concrete suggestions.

Both of these shifts are related to a fundamental transformation in how we consider ourselves in the world. Am I as an individual able to transform from a focus on my egoistic "me" perspective to embracing the larger "we," which includes every living being in the world? Or, alternatively, as an organization, are we able to overcome our natural habit of competition to experience the benefits of co-creation with parties we have never before worked with? The two mindset transformations are required

DOI:10.4324/9781003305941-11

to ensure that individual leaders and the organizations can overcome an inward-looking closed perspective that prevents working together with those who hold different opinions.

These mindset transformations have been proven as predictors for organizational change. This means that if an organization has both a leader or a leadership team with an outside-in leadership mindset and a co-creative organizational mindset, it is only a question of time until the organization reorients itself to embrace a broader role in society and starts generating positive value for society and the planet – and this is a great source for hope.

9 The transformation from "me" to "we"

Short story: the Swedish activist finds the courage to trust the enemy

Do you remember the case study in Part I about the occupation of the Swedish hospital? Local activists rebelled against a local government decision to close down the maternity ward of their region. The activist leader was justifiably irritated and felt pushed into a highly defensive position. He was not only disillusioned about receiving government support, he strongly distrusted anybody in government. Nonetheless, he was set to keep the maternity ward open and for this he needed to work with the government. He initiated an occupation of the hospital to have the attention of the government officials. It was a powerful move and had resulted in the government officials not being re-elected. The newly elected government official had promised during the election campaign to enter into a dialogue with the activists. While this represented a success for the activists, they faced their own challenge for the next phase. Would they be able to trust the new government official to engage on their end in a dialogue?

My colleague, Bernard le Roux, of the Leadership for Transition team was among the mediators, and he recalls the development process of the activist leader. He describes what happened with the activist leader as an act of unfreezing from a deep fear and distrust of the government representatives. The activist leader would slowly be able to see the government official as an actual person who was more than a representative of an institution. Seeing the human instead of the role the person represented enabled the activist to recognize that he projected his fear onto the person without seeing the actual human in front of him. It took the mediators numerous personal discussions with the activist leader to reach that stage. It also required similar such

DOI:10.4324/9781003305941-12

meetings with the government representatives who faced issues of trust and collaboration on their side, too.

Ultimately, the external pressure certainly helped. If the activist leader wanted to achieve what he was set to accomplish, he had no other choice than to sit down with the government representative and to advance enough trust to believe that something good could come out of such a talk. How did he accomplish this? Initially, when he opted to occupy the hospital, he reached out to as many allies as possible to help with the occupation. This resulted in a strengthening of his position and created a transformation from being alone in this (a "me" stance) to a sense of being aligned with others and doing something right "for us" together. This resulted in a change in government and an opportunity to be taken seriously. It illustrates one of the transformation pathways that enables somebody to transformation from a "me" to a "we" stance.

Opening up to be connected with all that is

Let us explore the transformation challenge of an individual so that she or he can embrace a "we" instead of a "me" mindset. A "we" mindset is required to effectively collaborate with others and to work on solutions that serve more than only one's personal interest. It is also a mindset needed to overcome polarized conflicts. The transformation from the "me" to the "we" stance relates to how a person defines her or his identity: Who am I? Am I a single isolated being or do I experience myself as being a part of a larger community, the world, all life? The broader we define our identity, the greater the chance of finding a common ground with others. Recognizing multiple belongings creates bridges, research confirms.[1]

Having studied the leaders of Positive Impact Organizations, we learned more about the transformation from "me" to "we." These insights build on my book entitled "The Five Superpowers."[2] While there are likely to be many transformation journeys, it may help portray them as two transformational challenges. One happens within and the other one can be observed more easily from the outside.

The first challenge relates to an inner development of the person. At one extreme, egocentric or narcissistic persons typically experience themselves as entirely disconnected from the world. To them, their entire experience is all about themselves, and little else matters. This is what we call an extreme "me" stance. At the other end of the spectrum, people having suffered tragedies or traumas may end up being introverted, and experience the world as a threat and themselves as victims. They also suffer from a great sense of being disconnected, albeit for different reasons than a narcissist. While the inner journey is clearly different – one finds a pathway to regain trust, the other to resize the individual's ego such that she or he experiences herself or himself as part of the world – both will lead to defining the person as an important, small, and meaningful part of the world, just like any other living sentient being present in the universe. This transformation can occur in many manners. A meaningful experience in nature appears to be particularly effective in finding such a connection. To me, it is the time I spend hiking in the mountains, where I feel this sense of being totally connected with everything that is and where I sense that a tree is as much a part of me as I am a part of the mountain I walk on. This first inner challenge is expressed in the stance a person takes in life.

The second challenge of an individual mindset transformation is about how the person acts externally. Others will be able to observe this more easily. You can ask yourself: How open or closed is the person? An externally open person makes you feel welcome and heard. The person will proactively seek to hear the opinions of others and focuses on consolidating different perspectives in an attempt to find common ground. It is often the role of a facilitator to assume such an inclusive approach. When, at the other end of the spectrum, a person is closed and self-focused, it is likely that the person will not seek out the divergent views of others and may even attempt to shut them down. This can be expressed silently or vocally, depending on the personality. It takes enormous courage to step up from being closed to being open. In my experience, nobody is entirely the one or the other. The externally visible behavior depends a lot on the situation, on whether the person has something to lose or to gain, and how viscerally important the outcome is.

These two transformation challenges hopefully provide, to a certain extent, granularity about the process. Let us remember that there is no black and white in transformation; a lot depends on the issue and the context. There are situations in which most of us tend to be egoistic and closed. The invitation here is to find spaces where we can feel connected with all life and, consequently, to be open to others.

Embracing a larger purpose

Having explored the transformation challenges, let us highlight three pathways of how to actually achieve this transformation from a "me" mindset to and a "we" mindset (see also Figure 9.1).

For ourselves: A pathway of moving beyond a "me" focus can consist of joining a movement or group that defends a special issue you care about. The sense of community that grows from standing up for a common issue is rich and very real. It may serve as a stepping stone to recognizing that the higher truth of the "we" includes all of us. Such a transformation may occur when an individual witnesses the solution of an issue that satisfies several parties. This is in many respects the secret spark of any positive compromise that was achieved by having found a shared higher purpose.

The quantum leap: A number of people experience an enlightenment and suddenly understand it. I am not joking. I know of several persons who have had an experience in their life that has fundamentally transformed them to

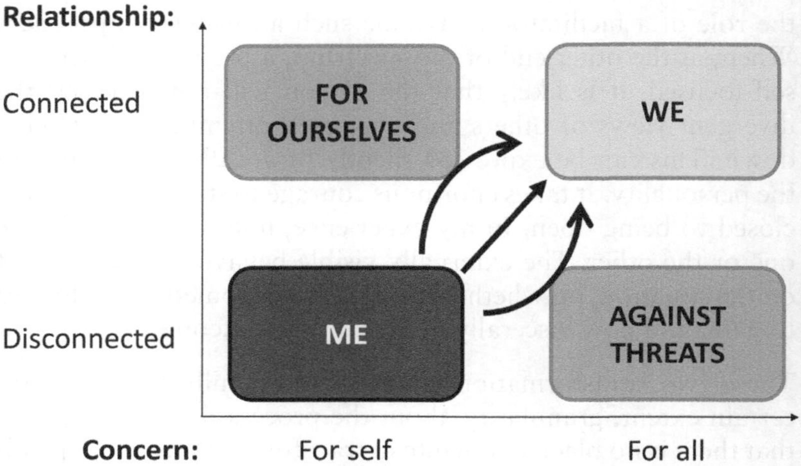

Figure 9.1 Three transformation pathways for individuals

instantly and immediately understand the "we." Please do not misunderstand me, these are not semi-gods or buddhas; these are persons who have consistently been able to put the common good above their own personal interest. They are not flawless beings and there are instances during which they may fall back into a "me" stance. Fear can be such a negative trigger. And yet, I am sure, you have also had an experience where it was easy to help achieve the best interest for the group rather than fighting for your own preference. Most people who grew up in families or communes have likely had, to a certain extent, healthy exposure to this pathway.

Against threats: The third transformation pathway resembles the first pathway. Here, rather than experiencing the benefits of a group that resembles us, we experience the benefits of a highly diverse group that is united by opposing the same threat. The group exists because together they are stronger. We may have to overcome preconceived notions about other participants in the group so that we can actually work together. We may have to pause our mental framing and grant others their space, as otherwise the threat cannot be handled. It is a coalition of emergency and need and it works well in overcoming the "me" and in experiencing the "we." Being able to identify an ideal future that includes the visions of everybody around the table, an individual can experience a moment where her or his concern is addressed (the threat is potentially gone) while others also find peace in the solution. A new shared "we" is created.

There is no best path. Every individual has a different starting point. Such a starting point is a reflection of the individual's personal history. And the path depends on what current reality the individual faces.

Should the question ever arise whether there is a method to measure a mindset, there may be a tool that can help shed light, to a certain extent, on the inner state and potentially highlight a number of blind spots. The Competency Assessment for Responsible Leadership (CARL) may help create an inner awareness of which path may be more appropriate for the individual. The CARL was designed to be used for individuals, teams, and

Degree of mastery (columns) Competency dimensions (rows)	***Knowing (Knowledge)***	***Doing (Skills)***	***Being (Attitudes)***	% of max
Stakeholder relations	3	2	3	67
Ethics and values	2	2	1	40
Self-awareness	2	3	4	79
Systems understanding	2	3	3	69
Change and innovation	4	4	3	90
% of max	65	70	70	

CARL score: 69

4 = competency appears very mature and well developed - congratulations!
3 = competency appears developed and approaches maturity, with minor areas to possibly improve
2 = competency is in development and has important potential for improvement
1 = competency is underdeveloped and there is significant opportunity for improvement

Figure 9.2 The Competency Assessment for Responsible Leadership (CARL)

organizations to assess their degree of responsibility in their leadership and decision making. Responsibility is defined as the ability to see beyond one's self-interest and to effectively work with others and within oneself to uncover solutions that serve a higher purpose. It builds on five competencies including handling stakeholder relations, ethics and values, self-awareness, systems understanding, and change and innovation.3 The CARL assesses a person's knowledge, skills, and attitudes in each of these five competencies, offering a uniquely granular view of where one has potential to further develop. (See Figure 9.2).

The five competency dimensions offer insights into what competencies can be built on and which may prevent a fruitful collaboration. On the other axis, the three action dimensions, i.e., knowing, doing, and being, highlight the way in which a given competency can be used or improved. The CARL test is free and a code can be obtained so that a group of any size can create a profile of a department or organization (more here: www.carl2030.org).

Notes

1 Shafak, E. (2020): *How to Stay Sane in an Age of Division*. London: Wellcome Collection, p. 41.

2 Muff, K. (2018). *The Five Superpowers of Co-creators*. Sheffield: Routledge.
3 Muff, K., Liechti, A., and Dyllick, T. (2020): How to apply responsible leadership theory in practice – A competency tool to collaborate on the sustainable development goals. *Corporate Social Responsibility and Environment CSRaEM Journal*, 27–5, 2254–2274.

10 Unpacking the individual mindset transformation

Short story: U.S. NGOs find pathways to bridge polarization

In a country where polarization is painfully visible in politics, it takes courage to invest in solutions that bridge the profound differences between the two main parties, i.e., the Democrats and Republicans. In 2016, a group of American Democrats and Republicans created an association they call Brave Angels.[1] The purpose of the association is to bridge the political divide. The Brave Angels use methods that were developed for marriage therapy and organized online workshops for Democrats and Republicans. Their promise is simple: Join us for a workshop where nobody will convince the other about anything. This promise sets the stage for people in the workshop to agree that the only thing they talk about is themselves.

In a first session, Democrat and Republican participants work in separate groups and start by identifying common prejudices about their own party. Then, they reflect among themselves which of these prejudices contain a spark of truth. In a second session, Democrat and Republican participants work in a joint session where they can ask members of the other party questions; questions that are real and answerable rather than suggestive or leading. Each question can be answered by one person. It is suggested that the response includes a personal story and focuses on being honest and transparent. As in marriage therapy, the purpose of these workshops is to listen to each other, to let the other speak without interrupting. The purpose is to identify commonalities and to avoid generalizations.

This process shows a pathway for transforming from "me" to "we." The first session establishes an awareness that serves to build trust and therefore enables a deeper reflection on one's own position. In a second step, participants are invited to

DOI:10.4324/9781003305941-13

experience the "we" through the storytelling of the others. Certain stories may resonate with our personal stories, hence reducing the sense of otherness.

Brave Angels have held hundreds of such workshops across the United States, both in person and online. The interest in such events has increased so much that the organizers allow up to 50 silent participants to listen into the conversations. Brave Angels are not alone in their attempt to bridge polarization and reconcile the United States. Make America Dinner Again is an organization that invites Republicans and Democrats for a shared dinner. The host cooks and a moderator is present and ensures that the eight to ten participants honor the rules of the game. These include not interrupting each other, and that each statement is expressed in the "I" form to avoid generalizations. There is a time-out bell when discussions become too heated, allowing everybody to take a deep breath. Since 2016, more than 200 such dinners have taken place across the country.

These outline two examples of how we can loosen the grip on the "me" and how we can shift toward the "we." This is achieved by making the conversation personal through the use of personal stories that we share and listen to. When we make a connection with somebody else, things change and we can step beyond the "me." It is our mind and our thoughts that can drag us back to our "me" stance, while it is the heart, deeper in the body, that reaches for connection. While it is certainly easier to make a connection face to face, for example, by cooking together, it is also possible to realize this connection online as is demonstrated so beautifully in the Brave Angels story.

Insights on the individual mindset transformation

Jason Jay, Director of the Sustainability Initiative at MIT Sloan, and Gabriel Grant wrote the book entitled "Breaking through gridlock," which invites readers to join a journey of overcoming polarization in conversations.[2] The two authors have understood the additional efforts required in addressing polarized as opposed to classic conflicts. They offer interesting insights in how to accomplish this shift from "me" to "we." They start by redefining what authenticity means in a conversation. Often, authenticity is all about being consistent with what I have said before, or how I have behaved in the past. Such a static definition of authenticity often results in stuck conversations. Jason Jay and Gabriel Grant point to a dynamic interpretation of authenticity whereby people share their story and their perspectives, instead of just speaking their mind and sharing a prefabricated opinion. This approach was used by the Brave Angels in theprevious story. Sharing personal stories instead of generalizing is what opens up the space and builds a foundation of trust so that we can listen to each other. The authors point out that such personal stories are able to weaken polarized certainties and help create a shared sense of vulnerability and potential openness to learning.

The "me" to "we" transformation is also of central concern to Jason Jay and Gabriel Grant. They developed a Spheres-of-Care model to frame attempts of broadening the perspective and shifting a polarized conflict to a higher level. Their model helps parties understand where their perspective is located. In increasingly large circles, they define the shift from a "me" to "all life," with "me" being the smallest circle, followed by a next circle called "immediate relationships," followed by other circles respectively called "organization," "community," "nation," "humanity," "future generations," and ultimately ending with the largest circle that encompasses all other circles: "all life." The model illustrates the shift from "me" to "we."

The two authors offer concrete advice on how to reach this higher ground. Their proven process helps participants become unstuck from conversations between two polarized perspectives. Using the example of a sustainability expert trying to convince a chief financial officer (CFO) to assess investments not just from a financial perspective but to also consider the environmental and social impact of corporate investment choices, they suggest the following:

- Start by acknowledging the dilemma and the contradiction of the two perspectives.
- Help build a shared understanding by describing the two perspectives as clearly as possible.
- Validate the two perspectives with solid examples of both perspectives, and show that this is a one-dimensional approach of either-or, i.e., a trade-off.

- Suggest an innovation space beyond the one-dimensional trade-off situation, pointing out a new dimension with opportunities beyond this either-or space.
- Invite the other person to consider solutions in the both-and innovation space and explore options together in this two-dimensional space.

In their example, the sustainability expert and the CFO ended up agreeing to explore data which traditional investors ignored. This approach was followed to assess if such information might highlight new opportunities. They studied both the emerging new environmental, social, and governance (ESG) data as well as impact data from smaller providers. Together, they identified additional investment opportunities that satisfied both the financial as well as the broader sustainability requirements.

When we studied the challenges that individuals would encounter during multistakeholder processes, we identified a similar insight. We identified opposing strength polarities that triggered unavoidable tensions.[3] Most of these tensions did not qualify as polarized conflicts; they were essentially standard classic conflicts that could be resolved without the need to find a higher common ground. What we had discovered, however, is that classic conflicts can be resolved more easily when the two parties at conflict are able to realize that both sides operate from a perspective that is of value. I called it an overstretched strength. By studying the original underlying strength and by exploring a combination of these two underlying strengths that were in conflict, we pointed out that a superpower could be found. This proved enormously helpful in these situations of conflict.

For example, somebody with a critical mindset would challenge solutions of somebody with a positive mindset. When these two would start considering their positions as "either-or" cases, conversations became stuck. We had discovered that we could help them move beyond the one-dimensional space by recognizing that both perspectives rooted in important competencies that strengthened the overall process. Combining a critical and a positive mindset would land the parties in a two-dimensional space of appreciation, where ideas were valued from both a critical and a positive perspective. See Figure 10.1.

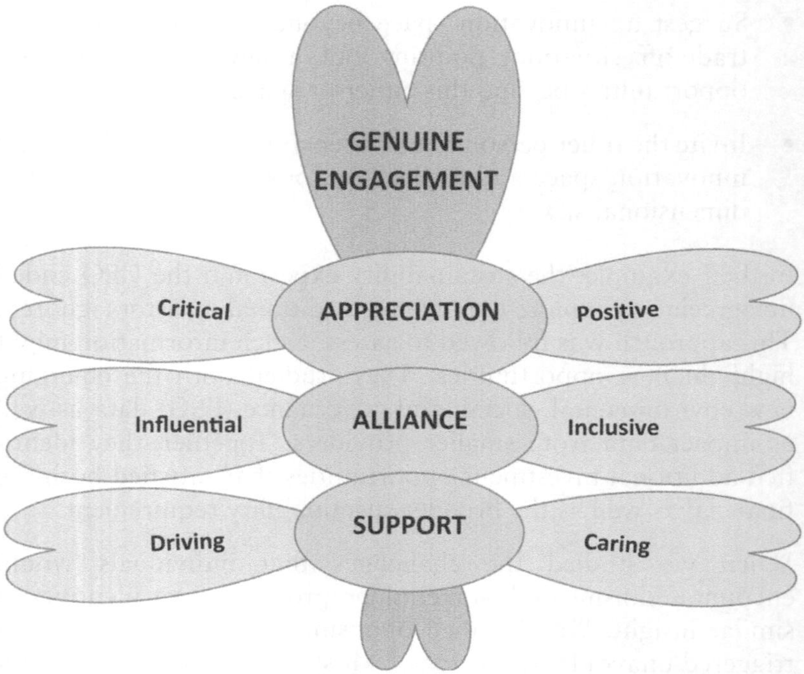

Figure 10.1 Overview of the individual strength polarities and higher-level superpowers

Source: Courtesy of the Five Superpowers for Co-creators Book

Similarly, we had uncovered that when a person insists on featuring only influential voices and another person wants to ensure that everybody is heard instead, there is a new higher ground for an alliance between unique voices of influence with the colorful voices of inclusion. All that is required, is simply for somebody to point out this opportunity to search for an alliance and for new perspectives that open up in this light.

A frequent conflict occurred when a particularly driven participant encountered a participant who strongly cared about a certain subset of activities. The two sides would end up digging in their heels insisting that the process was either too slow or too fast, losing valuable time and energy arguing. We managed to unblock such situations by having both parties feeling recognized that their point is valid and important, and that they could explore different avenues to support the apparently minor issue in a more effective and speedy manner by brainstorming alternative pathways. This new dimension enabled both participants to step into their strengths, to quickly highlight a suitable solution, and to move on.

You might find yourself in a situation where you hear two people arguing, too. Rather than taking a side, why not highlight the underlying strength that lies hidden behind each position and describe these so that they are valued and recognized? This is a first step to figuring out what the combination of both positions may be like in the innovation space that opens up when we move from the one-dimensional conflict to the two-dimensional space of opportunities and shared values. This is what a superpower is all about.

Moving beyond the ego focus

Does this mean that classic and polarized conflicts can be resolved in the same manner? No. I would suggest solving any conflict in the easiest and most direct manner possible. Classic conflicts can often be overcome by identifying a win-win outcome to the involved parties, with the win-win outcome not requiring them to first connect at a personal level. Polarized conflicts, however, are harder to resolve, as the people involved operate from different realities, which first need to be put aside and be overcome. We have observed that establishing a human connection is an excellent pathway for this.

In our current times, there is an increase in polarized conflicts. Everybody appears to be entitled to their own individual truth. Media has lost much of its hard-earned credibility and is questioned as soon as it does not report what the readers believe to be true. It appears that the right to one's own truth is becoming an individual right. Irrespective of what we think of this development, and how dangerous the spreading of disinformation and fake news is, we have to accept it as real. This new reality means that everybody can have their own truth.

In such a context, it is important to note that narcissism is no longer just an individual trait; it becomes a collective trait and such a collective trait can easily lead us to a false sense of recognizing our truth everywhere and in everything. Our truth becomes the center of our world, and any other truth is wrong. Political scientist and writer, Elif Shafak, points out that group narcissism is a compensation for personal frustrations, flaws, or failures.[4] The resulting inflated belief can result in a clear-cut sense of us versus them, and such a conviction easily leads to a resentment toward those believing in alternative truths.

This is where the hard work is needed: For each of us who is caught up in this us versus them division, a transformation opportunity awaits – an opportunity to step beyond a single perspective, a single truth, an invitation to seek a larger reality, a higher ground where the realities of all those around us can co-exist. It is not that we must agree with all those other perspectives, and it is also not that we must change them. The transformation is about acknowledging other perspectives and truths, and about welcoming to the table the person who thinks differently. It is about including the person first and foremost, and about accepting that they bring whatever reality is theirs.

Robert Cialdini, behavioral scientist and former adviser of President Obama, confirms the importance of respecting the position of those who think differently than us. He suggests that they are as unlikely to change their minds as we are. He points out that there is no point in pressuring somebody to do something, as this will simply create resistance and resentment.

What about when the good of society requires a certain segment of citizens to amend their stance? Can the collective need override the individual need? Roberto Cialdini recommends honoring the individual freedom in deciding what is right and suggests to provide both new information and to frame such news as trends rather than isolated facts. In his experience, this is an effective approach to detach an individual from her or his preconceived opinion. Let us consider the concrete example of society benefitting from as many people as possible being vaccinated in Switzerland. When the resistance to vaccination grew, about 58% of the Swiss population were vaccinated. Sharing that number in isolation is not helpful. However, saying that three months prior 38% were vaccinated, two months prior 51%, and then actually 58%, changes things. Roberto Cialdini points out that people love to be a part of a growing trend. Hence, showing a growing trend shows how people around us act and this might help reframe our individual position. Such trends provide a larger picture that can help a person not only move beyond an ego focus but also want to be a part of an evolving society.[5]

Instead of changing others, do reach out to the other person and search beyond her or his individual perspective. Create a human connection and acknowledge that you see things differently. Confirm this reality with concrete examples and ensure that everybody in the room feel heard and acknowledged – and only then point out a joint journey to a two-dimensional innovation space where everybody together can explore opportunities beyond the "either or" to identify potential ideas that work in a "both and" world. There are three or more pathways to achieve that: by standing for our shared interest, by discovering a larger concern, or by a sheer aha moment. Furthermore, there are other pathways, too. Let us recognize where we start and where others start and let us connect with the person in front of us and take things from there. Expanding our range of care from just ourselves and our tribe to society and all life will enable us to step beyond the ego focus into a space where we can explore solutions beyond polarized opinions.

Notes

1 Langer, M.-A. (2020): Die Amerikaner gehen in die Selbsttherapie. *NZZ*, December 27, accessed online August 3, 2021: www.nzz.ch/international/graeben-in-den-usa-amerikaner-gehen-in-selbsttherapie-ld.1593051?reduced=true

2 Jay, J., and Grant, G. (2017): *Breaking Through Gridlock – The Power of Conversation in a Polarized World*. Oakland: Berret-Köhler.

3 Muff, K. (2018): *Five Superpowers for Co-creators – How Change Makers and Business Can Achieve the Sustainable Development Goals*. Sheffield: Routledge.

4 Shafak, E. (2020): *How to Stay Sane in an Age of Division*. London: Wellcome Collection, p. 19.

5 Fromme, C., and Wichert, S. (2021): Menschen werden eher aktiv, wenn es den persönlichen Interessen dient. *Tages Anzeiger*, September 25: https://epaper.tagesanzeiger.ch/#article/20/Tages%2DAnzeiger/2021-09-25/35/125131036

11 The transformation from competition to co-creation

Short story: the Swiss WWF becomes a partner for business

In the 90s, the World Wide Fund for Nature Switzerland (WWF) was mostly engaged in campaigning and had just started a number of convening activities. Convening activities included multistakeholder initiatives on sourcing paper or soy and involved the big Swiss retailers Migros and Coop. WWF soon realized that to make change happen, every initiative needed one major front-runner to pave the way. The NGO became involved by developing sector-specific ratings, outlining how the various industry players compared to their competitors. Such ratings served as incentive or as pressure for laggers to catch up and follow the frontrunners. The sustainable palm oil scorecard, for example, resulted in a few of the laggers starting to close the gap with the leaders, hence enabling the WWF to focus on the next topic they thought business needed to improve.

When the WWF started to engage with business, they encountered a perception risk. How can they work out solutions with business, and at the same time be a credible boundary-pusher? The WWF needed to ensure that they clearly separated their rating activities from their collaboration with the businesses. To do this, the WWF outsourced the rating activities to independent external consultants. As a result, they can commission topical ratings and work with business to close the gap.

Not all business sectors are as happy to work with the WWF as the Swiss retail sector. It takes a certain amount of consumer, investor, and political pressure for business to set more ambitious goals. Not all sectors face such pressure. While the awareness in retail and the food sector is significant, textile and jewelry sectors move slower. It is also essential to scientifically measure the required improvements in a core business

DOI:10.4324/9781003305941-14

so that the gap between the current and the ideal status can be highlighted clearly. This gap analysis then enables business to establish strategies with measurable and ambitious goals.

Such cross-sector collaboration has its challenges. It is not always easy to communicate complex issues in a punchy manner so that consumers understand. The example of growing strawberries in Spain highlights such a complexity. Southern Spain is an important fruit and vegetable provider for Europe and is known for treating immigrant workers poorly and exploiting the regional groundwater. Retailers that engage in systems to improve the production and transport transparency and the local working conditions face the challenge of communicating the slow progress that accompanies the resulting change. Another current food issue is the high climate impact of meat consumption. Obviously, for vegetarians and vegans it would be easiest to simply ban meat. Yet, there is also a space for sensitizing meat consumers to buy environmentally and socially responsible meat. The WWF has learned to broaden its approach and to incite its retail partners to develop transparent tools so that consumers can make better purchasing choices. This strategy requires a close collaboration with its business partners, building trust along the way. For example, the consumer tool, the M check, which Swiss retail giant Migros developed, is a result of such pressure and a good example to illustrate that the WWF can maintain its critical role as it collaborates with business.

The WWF is well aware of the challenging position it finds itself in by collaborating with business, the often-perceived public enemy. As a result, its due diligence efforts have increased, as the institution cannot afford to be seen as supporting green washing. Today, businesses in Switzerland appreciate the WWF as a well-respected partner. This was not always the case; business has for a long time been reticent to work with NGOs. In recent years, NGOs like the WWF that engaged in partnerships with future-oriented businesses provide an important contribution to solve the growing environmental and societal challenges.

Tanja Mächler, the Co-Head Corporate Relations at the WWF Switzerland, explored the previous story with me. The story provides an insightful example of how a cross-sector collaboration can work and how stakeholders on all fronts are challenged to amend their positions so that they are positive contributors. This relates not only to NGOs like the WWF but also to business and government.

Recognizing value in the difference of opinions

Not many organizations have experienced the positive effect of working with players across sectors as is showcased in the short story of the WWF and the Swiss retailers. For a long time, the WWF has considered business primarily as a source for funding their core activities focused on protecting wildlife and biodiversity. Nowadays, NGOs like the WWF understand that business can be both a creator and a resolver of environmental problems and have found means to collaborate with it. Business is sometimes reticent of NGOs and consider them as a threat. Organizations need to undergo a mindset transformation to move beyond such a competitive or defensive spirit. The challenge for organizations of any kind – be it a government, a not-for-profit organization, a startup, or a multinational – is to redefine their role and to look beyond their own interests to see value in contributing to the society in which they operate.

Our research into Positive Impact Organizations enabled us to understand what is involved in achieving such an organizational transformation. The transformation can be observed by the extent to which an organization has broadened its perspective regarding its stakeholders. In the past, business organizations have focused primarily on the interest of their owners or shareholders. Over the past two decades, many businesses have started to recognize value in engaging with a broader stakeholder group. Such stakeholders include their employees, their suppliers and sub-suppliers, as well as their clients, customers, and their end users. More recently, when attempting to contain their carbon footprint, advanced sustainability organizations engaged with stakeholders across the full value chain to close the loop of their product life cycle. In 2021, Unilever has requested its shareholders to approve its climate transition action plan, ensuring endorsement for such a broad engagement of all stakeholders.[1] The Unilever example illustrates a broader consideration of stakeholders and reflects an outside-in perspective of an organization.

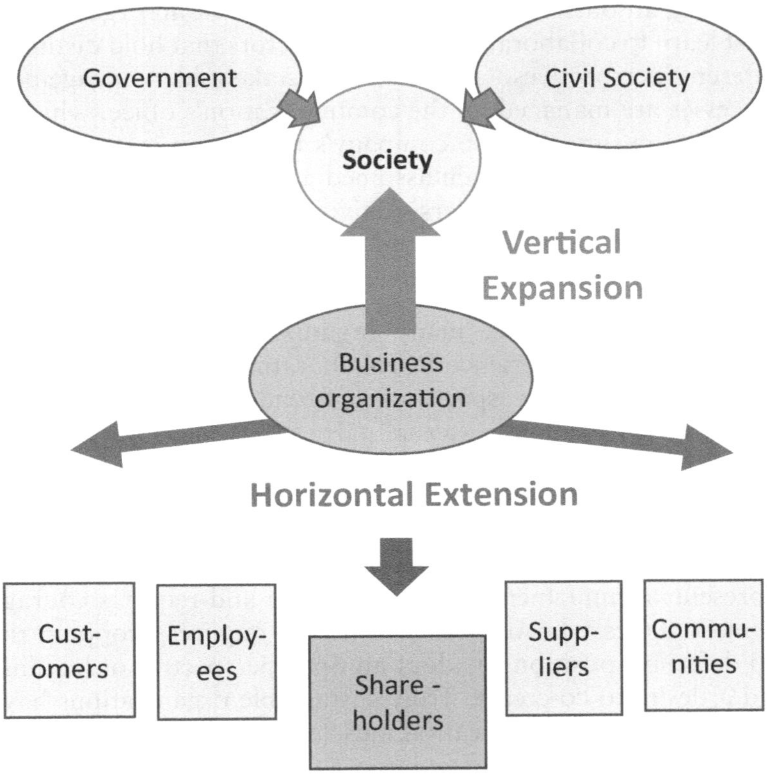

Figure 11.1 The changed role of business organizations in society
Source: Reproduced with permission from Dyllick-Muff 2021

A well-functioning society requires all of its active participants, all organizations, and all institutions, to consider themselves not in the traditional inside-out perspective but rather in the light of their role for society. The inside-out perspective locates an organization at the center of its universe. An outside-in perspective places an organization as one of the many players in a larger setting that serves society, and ultimately the planet. This outside-in perspective triggers a new awareness for organizations. In a first instance, an organization engages in a horizontal expansion to include all of its stakeholders beyond the traditional shareholder. In a second instance, the organization expands vertically and embraces the understanding that it is one of many stakeholders of society, with a role and a responsibility to society and our planet (see Figure 11.1).

Adopting an outside-in perspective means that an organization must learn to collaborate with societal actors that hold distinctly different perspectives. Traditionally, stakeholder engagement processes are managed by the communication's office, which is careful to ensure that the company's reputation is not at risk. As a result, they have often assumed a rather defensive attitude toward external stakeholders. Activists are well known for their critical if not aggressive attitude toward business, which are consequently often reluctant to engage with them.

Over the past decade, many organizations have benefitted from a positive experience in collaborating with stakeholders. This has opened the space for a broader and more diverse engagement with more external parties that often provide very different opinions and perspectives. The previous short story has illustrated the transformation of the WWF in Switzerland and how it has become an appreciated partner for many business organizations. Embracing the outside-in perspective represents a fundamental transformation and requires courage to meet actors who think differently; it requires dropping the old defensive position to adopt an open perspective of learning and a desire to co-create. Truly sustainable organizations have developed a strong co-creation muscle and are increasingly able to consider differences of opinion as opportunities to develop and grow. They consider such differences as insights into how they might develop new business models in areas thus far ignored. This muscle is called stakeholder co-creation and is based on the idea that a diversity of opinions in a room can result in new and better ideas. Positive Impact Organizations have learned that such co-creation leads to new business models with new services targeted at resolving the environmental and social issues of our times.

Embracing co-creation

In its updated Vision 2050 report, the World Business Council for Sustainable Business (WBCSD) highlights that mindset transformations are an essential part of the business transition. One of the mindset transformations the WBCSD recommends is called regenerative thinking. Such thinking includes that business has to move beyond a doing-no-harm mindset. The WBCSD points out that it is time to unlock the potential for

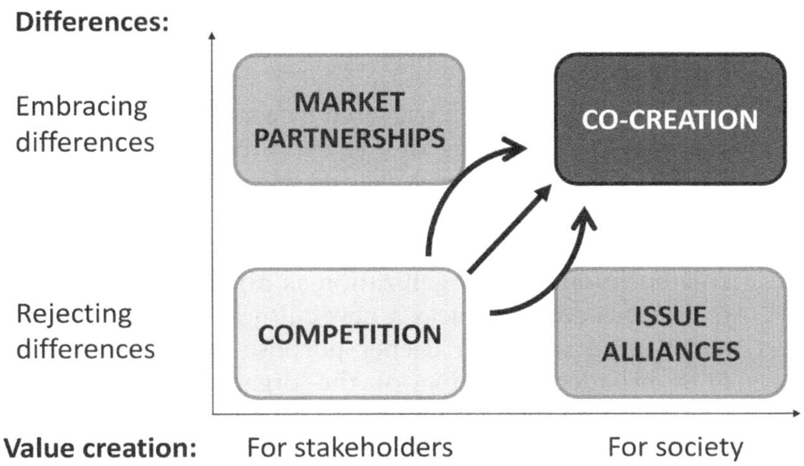

Figure 11.2 Three transformation pathways for organizations

resolving issues impacting the society and the planet, both of which business depends on. The influential WBCSD calls for business to build their capacity to regenerate, thrive, and evolve not just for its own sake but also to ensure a healthy society and planet.[2] This includes a collaboration with government, too.

Observing Positive Impact Organizations, which have embedded this approach, has allowed us to identify three pathways to transform from a state of competition to a state of co-creation.

The three pathways in Figure 11.2 suggest that an organization has several means of transforming its mindset. Let us explore these three identified pathways:

Market partnerships: An organization initiates it transformation by moving beyond a tribe focus that relies on trusted connections for partnerships with like-minded players in existing markets. When such new partnerships result in positive experiences, the organization builds on the resulting trust and is ready to reach beyond current business boundaries. For example, this can occur when members of the innovation department present new opportunities to management. The more beneficial such opportunities and business models are, the higher is the interest in reaching out even further to explore co-creation with new partners beyond current market players.

The quantum leap: Often triggered by a sudden aha moment, an influential member of the executive leadership team triggers a quantum leap transformation. They bring in entirely new ideas far from business-as-usual. New stories start circulating in the organization about such beneficial collaboration. The organization is able to let go of the tribe focus and embraces a new cultural logic. People feel encouraged to find a deeper purpose and new meaning in a broader definition of the organization's purpose. The organization attracts new talent that builds on this expanded sensemaking to define the organization as a part of society with an important role to play in it. Such a transformation can happen quite speedily.

Issue alliances: An organization may experience the benefits of collaboration by engaging with new players in a topical coalition. Such collaboration typically happens with little known, friendly players. For example, there may be a need to align to protect against an external market threat or pressure. The positive outcome of such a collaboration can create a foundation of trust to participate in further such alliances. Such efforts may be initiated by the chief strategy officer or the head of sustainability or somebody from business development. The more stories about the benefits of such collaboration circulate, the more employees will come forward with ideas for further alliances. The experience of benefits and opportunities of working on common solutions with new partners changes how the organization perceives itself.

These are three pathways we have observed at Positive Impact Organizations. There certainly are others. Every organization has a different starting point and a different culture and leadership team and will hence develop its own transformation path.

Organizational transformation is context and culture dependent. While the culture of an organization describes how the organization functions internally within its boundaries, the mindset of an organization highlights how the organization interacts externally within its larger, societal environment. The organizational culture and the organizational mindset are interconnected.

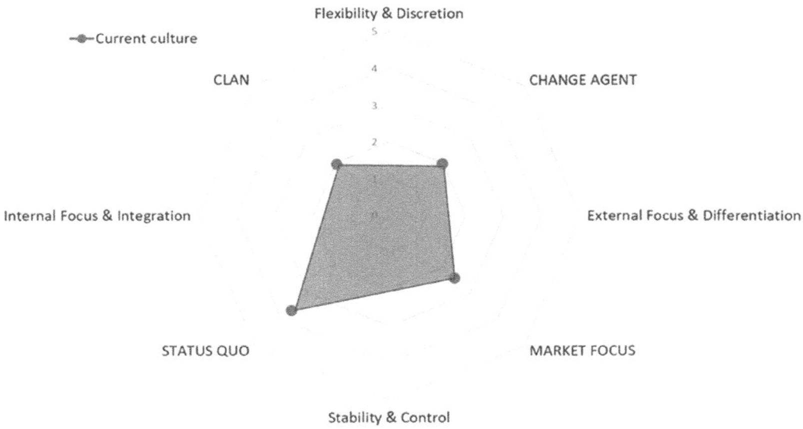

Figure 11.3 The change readiness assessment

Indeed, it is hard to imagine an externally open, co-creative organizational mindset in an internal culture that is highly hierarchical and fear based. The more openly and collaboratively an organization operates outside of its boundaries, the more comfortable with risks it will need to be internally. It appears that the more decentralized and self-organized an organization is, the easier it is for its members to be open and collaborative with external organizations.

The change readiness assessment provides a good overview of where an organization is from a culture perspective (See Figure 11.3). It highlights an organization's current culture as viewed by its employees on two axes: stability and control versus flexibility and discretion on the vertical axis; internal focus and integration versus external focus and differentiation on the horizontal axis. The more the organizational culture shifts to the top right "change agent" quadrant, the better the organizational culture will support a transformation to an outside-in perspective.

Notes

1 Univeler seeks shareholder approval for transition action plan – 14.12.2020, accessed online February 26, 2021: www.unilever.com/news/press-releases/2020/unilever-to-seek-shareholder-approval-for-transition-action-plan.html
2 WBCSD (2021): Vision 2050 – Time to transform, accessed online July 8, 2021: www.wbcsd.org/download/file/12180

12 Unpacking the organizational mindset transformation

Short story: a Swedish city brings co-creation to life

In the Swedish city of Eskilstuna, the local government was set to find solutions for safety and security challenges in various neighborhoods. Political leaders and government officials were equally concerned about the negative effect of segregated neighborhoods and a significant immigrant population. Safety and security became a top priority for the city. In 2020, an extensive public dialogue was initiated. For this, the government explored stakeholder engagement methods and opted to use the dialogue method. As a result, mixed stakeholder groups consisting of citizens, business actors, and local government representatives met to consider three relevant aspects of security: economic security, social security, and criminological security.

Initially, the participants across all sectors of society who contributed were surveyed to identify the topics to be discussed at the stakeholder co-creation sessions. The survey highlighted significant concerns about the existence of gangs and the risk of young men being recruited by them. The initial conversations among citizens, officials, business owners, and politicians explored the problem. As a result, the stakeholders identified two root causes. On the one hand, they identified a general lack of trust and coherence in the city. On the other hand, they pointed to the difficulty a number of parents were experiencing in effectively raising children in a culture that significantly differed from their own. Having identified the root causes in such an inclusive process prepared the ground to explore new solutions. An agreement was reached that it would be best for any new solution to be tested with those concerned instead of imposing it top-down as is usually the case with government solutions.

DOI:10.4324/9781003305941-15

The sessions were moderated by facilitators who created a trusting and effective dialogue space. One of the objectives of these dialogues was to identify and explore the different perspectives of the concerned parties. The facilitators pointed out an important design element in these co-creation dialogues: to hold off jumping to solutions and to first explore the causes and effects of the problem at hand. The process of speaking openly and listening to different perspectives enabled participants to deepen their understanding of the problems while sharing their perspectives with each other. In this space of open sharing, facilitators sensed how trust was built and the potential for change began to emerge. Neighbors spoke of the need for mutual support regarding parenting issues. Representatives of civil society and small businesses highlighted the difficulties involved with local government programs and the stigma related to social service projects. As a result, the stakeholder participants proposed working on a program to support parents, which would be run by citizens and be supported by NGOs. They also proposed that citizens rather than the local government would initiate neighborhood activities. The participants agreed to implement these projects in the months to come.

These proposals are astonishing in the Swedish context. While townhall meetings are a known feature in local politics, public dialogue is normally used only to seek the input of citizens to a problem government needs to solve. Everybody – government and citizens alike – expects that government will step up to solve the problem. This attitude has been reinforced by the Swedish public management idea, which considers citizens as customers and the authorities as service providers. For stakeholder groups to gather and to begin thinking in terms of "we" rather than "us and them" is a significant change to the status quo. It represents a major transformation from a dependency relationship where government is responsible for dealing with difficult issues, to a relationship where citizens take responsibility and perceive the local government and businesses as partners.

In Eskilstuna, the implementation is still ongoing. Thus far, there are signs that both the citizens and the local government assume a new-found shared responsibility in working and deciding together. This is a fragile and people-dependent process. The challenge for the local government is to open itself up to sharing power and welcoming a new level of collaboration with citizens even if this will impact their established processes. The facilitators have trained a team of volunteers across various government departments as impartial facilitators who can accompany this sensitive implementation process. These newly trained facilitators are taught to consider existing processes as sufficiently flexible and adaptive so that new shared decision making can be integrated and embraced by the existing government structures. This represents an important culture change in government. In the case of Eskilstuna, this culture change is supported by the government leadership and the politicians, who recognize the need for collaboration and inclusion. The government-internal facilitators are also trained to ensure that citizens can overcome their own struggles in becoming involved and engaged in the important conversations about problems that affect them. This transformation also requires a culture change of the involved citizens: Instead of being passive recipients of government decisions, they are empowered to participate and to act.

This is an encouraging example of how a government organization and involved citizens have embraced the journey toward co-creation. The success of this story is to a large degree due to the dialogue method chosen to approach the problem at hand. The story offers a concrete window into how an organization, in this case a city government, has transformed itself to reconsider its place and role in society in the context of emerging new problems. This story shows that an issue alliance can indeed change an organization's stance in how it collaborates with others, opening up new avenues of not only co-creating solutions but also involving external stakeholders in reshaping its internal decision-making processes and structures. One of my colleagues of the Leadership for Transition team, Bernard Le Roux, was among those facilitators and shared this story with me.

Insights on the organizational mindset transformation

Facilitators focus on creating spaces that favor change, and yet when and how change happens can never be entirely predicted.

The facilitators focus on creating enabling conditions and remain open to learning more in the present moment. Finding a solution for a polarized situation brings different facilitation challenges than overcoming a classic conflict. Both are important during multistakeholder sessions that seek to solve a complex issue.

Let us start by exploring classic conflicts that emerge in multistakeholder sessions. We can use lessons learned during our previous research of the Leadership for Transition team. Similarly to Chapter 10, I have outlined three of the most frequent such conflicts in my book on the five superpowers. The objective for organizational participants in multistakeholder processes is to develop collective solutions. That sounds easier than is imagined. There are all kinds of conflicts that obstruct the process of finding collective solutions.

For one, there is an inherent tension between an efficient process whereby work is organized into expert teams and a need for participants to learn to develop new solutions with others. This efficacy versus sharing tension will sooner or later arise. We have learned to recognize both opposing polarities of this tension as a strength. We suggest that participants engaged in fighting this tension find a way to combine the two underlying strengths in service of identifying means to develop mastery. Mastery involves both teaching and learning; it includes outlining why things are done in a certain manner and practicing the set of skills. This means carefully balancing a desire for efficacy with the need to share and learn, and framing it with the goal to develop mastery. As a result, it is possible to have opposing parties find purpose in the superpower of mastery.

Similarly, we have observed the tension between a desire for a diversified research approach and the idea of prototyping solutions. It is a fight of assumptions of how to best develop future solutions. Obviously, both sides speculate. Since both sides care about the solution and about obtaining relevant results, it is relatively easy to point out that what it takes is a spirit of collaboration, of thinking forward together, that will be most likely to secure the solution everybody wants. Collaboration in this case becomes the superpower of uniting the two underlying strengths, i.e., multiplicity and prototyping.

There is another frequent conflict in such sessions that is worth exploring; it relates to how the problem is to be solved. There is the engineering approach, which dictates that a problem must be analyzed in all necessary detail so that it can be understood and then solved, and there is Otto Scharmer's popular Theory U, which dictates that any future-relevant solution must come from an imagined ideal future. These are fundamentally different approaches to solving a problem and they can break down a multistakeholder process. Having both parties agree that both approaches are valid is an important start. Thereafter, the superpower of deep search serves to suggests the power of both will eventually loosen up tight positions back into a spirit of finding collective solutions together. Figure 12.1 illustrates these three characteristic problems that organizations face when collaborating.

Now, let us delve into solving polarized conflicts. The Israeli-Palestine conflict has been a global conflict hotspot. It provides

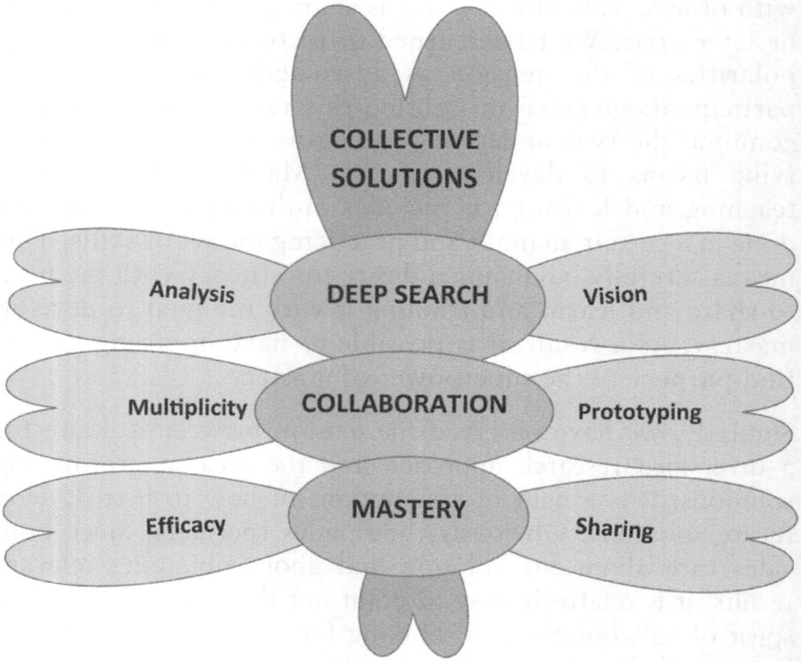

Figure 12.1 Overview of the organizational strength polarities and higher-level superpowers

Source: Courtesy of the Five Superpowers for Co-creators Book

relevant learning, given that it represents a situation with both sides having well defined positions. Polarization is fully in play, with both sides experiencing mutually exclusive realities. Ifat Maoz of the University of Hebrew, University of Jerusalem wanted to learn what would happen when Israeli and Palestinian teenagers meet to discuss social, cultural, and political topics.[1] He convinced an Israeli-Palestinian organization to initiate a series of two-day workshops. Each of the workshops was facilitated and included 40 highschoolers, about 20 from each side. The workshops featured activities and practices of transformative dialogues. Ifat Maoz observed five workshops and compared the perceptions, attitudes, and stereotypes held by the Jewish-Israeli and Palestinian teenagers both before and after a workshop. The changes before and after were so significant that they demonstrate the effectiveness of the workshops. Transformative practices imply the use of a forum of conversations, and represents a version of dialogue practices. Dialogue proves to be effective even in the context of a violent conflictual sociopolitical reality present between Israel and Palestine. The example shows that careful facilitated dialogue between groups with polarized positions can result in an improvement of attitudes. When people connect and engage in a dialogue, magic can happen.

The Israeli-Palestine example also shows that the method of engagement matters. Careful facilitation is an essential part and dialogue-based methods work better than debates or even deliberations. This has to do with each method having a different objective. In dialogues, the act of conversing is more important than the points made or the topic chosen. The focus of a dialogue lies on fostering the human connection, building or strengthening a relationship, and ideally reaching a mutual feeling of understanding.

In a debate, the parties hold opposing views and attempt to convince each other. Instead of focusing on the conversation itself as is the case with dialogue, in a debate it is the outcome that matters. In a debate, there is always a connotation of winning and losing and the competitive spirit is high.

Deliberations are normally used as a means to involve citizens in policy-making processes. A citizens' assembly is a common form of deliberation. It involves a selected group of citizens to speak about a specific policy challenge, and to deliberate on possible courses of action. Interestingly, such deliberations do not provide the same opportunity for a mindset transformation as dialogues generate. It has been observed that in deliberations, people become even more convinced of their views. They tend to counterargue the contrary arguments while uncritically accepting supporting arguments. People seek out evidence that confirms their thinking. Both of these biases result in a further polarization of people's attitude. This is especially true for those with the strongest ingoing opinions and of the highest levels of political sophistication.[2] Deliberating arguments from different points of view does not contribute to people changing their minds. People care too much about their reputation and their self-conception to be seen as being influenced.[3]

The method of engagement matters and shapes the outcome of any conflict – in polarized situations even more than in classic conflicts. The story about the Swedish city has illustrated this as well. If we want to reduce biases and seek to create enabling conditions for a potential mindset transformation, we must choose a suitable method. There are a variety of dialogue-based methods that work well. However, beware of debates and simple deliberations, as these just fortify opinions the parties had already made.

Moving beyond a competitive spirit

The mindset transformation for groups and organizations is all about stepping beyond a sense of competition and embracing a sense of co-creation. As the examples of polarized and classic conflicts have shown, this is easier said than done. The sense of competition is hard-wired in us and is visible in how organizations and political parties behave. Negotiations are about winning and losing. If necessary, it involves giving in now to be able to gain something later, about owing the other side or having a favor to call in.

American journalist and political analyst Ezra Klein studied the underlying causes of the U.S. polarization.[4] In his opinion, polarization will not disappear and has become a reality we have to live with. He appeals to our capacity to be tolerant. And yet, tolerance is incredibly hard when we are in a competitive mode. Ezra Klein points out that this sense of competition and polarization means that we need to reinforce our institutions and democracy in such a manner that they will not be broken by polarization.

An approach to help safeguard our democracies is to find approaches to include citizens in prioritizing and solving society's issues. The benefit of inviting a diversity of relevant voices into a room have been described in the Eskilstuna city story. It will be important to find methods to scale such micro cells of successful cross-partisan collaboration. The European Union tests this in various settings.[5] In Europe, there is indeed a growing appetite to include bottom-up citizen-based approaches to ensure that all voices are heard when new legislation is drafted. And yet, in Europe as in the United States and elsewhere, we have to accept that polarization is likely to stay.

We have explored that the method of engaging with multistakeholders matters. The various forms of dialogue provide the best results when comparing them to forms of deliberations and debate. Quantum theorist, David Bohm, has the theory behind why dialogues work to move beyond ego and competition to a sense of a shared purpose and co-creation.[6] The Bohm Dialogue is a method for co-creation dialogue groups to overcome the isolation of individuals and the fragmentation of society. The Bohm Dialogue builds on the idea of providing an equal status and free space to participants. David Bohm has identified these two elements as critical prerequisites of true communication. He points out that equal status and free space allow the appreciation of differing personal beliefs. In the Bohm Dialogue, participants are not allowed to interrupt each other, the person who speaks holding a speaking stone until they have said what they wanted. The simple fact of being able to speak without interruption and until it is all said, is transformative. Non-violent communication builds on this same experience. This simple rule forces listeners to suspend any immediate reaction or judgment. As a result, they hear their own reaction in their head and become aware of their potentially flawed and judgmental thought process. To extend this self-reflection, it is suggested that once the speaking stone is put down, that everybody takes a moment to pause. Then, rather than following a certain order to speak, the person who feels moved to speak grabs the stone and starts sharing. If you have ever participated in such a dialogue, you will have experienced the palpitations of your racing heart indicating that it is your time to speak.

Interestingly, there are digital experiments that create such dialogues. Vox Pop, a Dutch startup, has built a digital civic engagement platform solution that allows anonymous peer-to-peer discussions.[7] Their online political speed dating seeks to break the filter bubble in which we only hear what we want to hear. Vox Pop's objective is to bring the political debate closer to people. Its digital platform is built on a number of key principles such as one-on-one dialogues to sidestep the social desirability bias. The digital platform also features dialogues based on well-curated and provoking statements. In 2017, the Vox Pop tool has been used ahead of the Dutch, German, and Spanish elections and has enabled more than 35,000 such dialogues in a period of three to four weeks. In 2021, more than 300,000 Dutch citizens used the tool. Vox Pop enabled the need to break out of their bubble and to have such one-on-one dialogues with people of different political views. This appetite to learn about how others think is a promising indicator that the sense of competition can be put aside for a sense of co-creation to emerge.

Part III of this book considered in detail how to enable the individual and the organizational mindset transformations. For an individual, the challenge is to let go of the ego focus that comes along with a "me" mindset to embrace the larger purpose that serves all of us, the "we" mindset. For groups and organizations, it is about recognizing that we must pause our built-in sense of competition at times and embrace the truth that we are not the center of the universe. It means understanding that to create a just and sustainable world for all, we need to co-create with those who hold different views to us. This expansion of the model introduced in Part I and further developed in Part II now offers a complete overview of how polarized conflicts differ from classic conflicts. We have explored the different pathways of addressing both types of conflicts and what it takes to embrace the mindset transformation that allows us to shift from one approach to the other (see Figure 12.2).

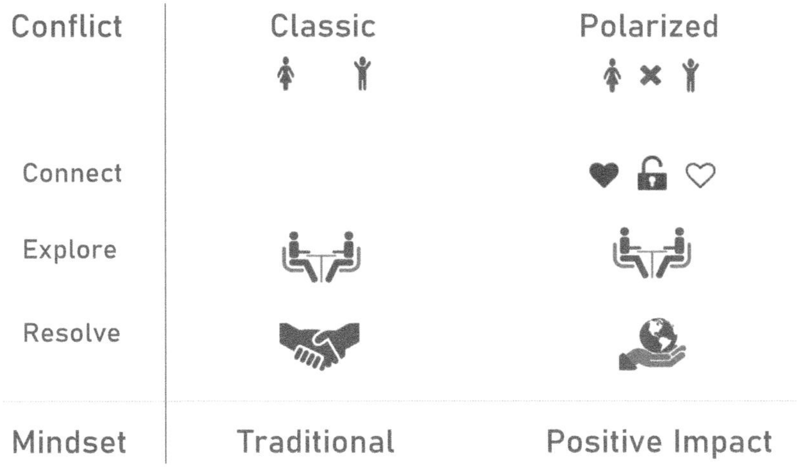

Figure 12.2 The classic vs. polarized conflict model in context of the mindset transformation

Notes

1 Maoz, I. (2000): An experiment in peace: Reconciliation-aimed workshops of Jewish-Israeli and Palestinian Youth. *Journal of Peace Research*, 37–6, 721–736.
2 Taber, C.S., and Lodge, M. (2006): Motivated skepticism in the evaluation of political beliefs. *American Journal of Political Science*, 50–3, 755–769.
3 Sunstein, C.R. (2002): *The Law of Group Polarization. The Journal of Political Philosophy*, 10–2, 175–195.
4 Klein, E. (2020): *Why We're Polarized*. London: Profile Books.
5 European Citizen Assemblies: https://citizensassemblies.org/european/
6 Bohm, D. (1993). The Undivided Universe: An Ontological Interpretation of Quantum Theory. Published post-humously.
7 Vox Pro: www.civinc.co/about

Part IV

The positive impact mindset

Part IV brings it all together and provides stories that showcase different aspects of the positive impact mindset. It also highlights further insights from research and develops concrete recommendations on how to go about creating the right mindset so that individuals and organizations can bring about positive change. Part IV connects these mindsets to the requirements of working together in Collaboratories, multistakeholder processes that are issue centered.

In an era where people doubt government and media alike, creating a valid foundation of trust among a diverse group of stakeholders becomes increasingly important. Business and NGOs are expected to provide societal leadership where government may no longer have the capacity or reach to do so. This demands a significant step change for business, which is challenged to create value not just for its shareholders but for society and the planet at large. This requires shifting from an inside-out perspective to an outside-in perspective. We have identified the mindsets that relate to the inside-out perspective as the "me" mindset at the individual level and the competition mindset at the organizational level. It is about stopping to worry about the risks that sustainability challenges pose to integrating the sustainability issues into a purpose-oriented strategic innovation process – and such a perspective is founded in a positive impact mindset.

We bring together insights developed thus far to generate the need for a shared higher purpose when working together across polarization so that complex societal issues can be solved. This includes creating a space where people of different origins of mind, background, expectations, and perspectives can engage in a dialogue. It is about re-creating trust and re-building a human connection. We also summarize and enrich the pathways for

DOI:10.4324/9781003305941-16

transforming from a traditional mindset to a positive impact mindset, highlighting insights at the individual and the organizational challenges from both practice and research.

Working together in uncertain times that often involve complex polarized conflicts requires a strong capacity to hold the tension that occurs when things do not proceed as planned. This brings additional challenges for the facilitation process of such multistakeholder processes. We consider important aspects of these challenges and provide hands-on recommendations for facilitators. We close with a number of personal recommendations for leaders and change makers, pointing out challenges that are likely to occur in their journey. The suggestions seek to provide the necessary awareness to enable an open and flexible mind. This is in the interest of working together in a collaborative space where everybody's perspective can be heard and where the spirit of a larger shared purpose ultimately wins the day. It is a journey that takes much courage, awareness, compassion, and patience.

13 The foundation of shared purpose co-creation

Short story: the Dutch Academy Director finds the higher ground

Berit Ann Roos, the director of an academy of architecture in the Netherlands, was put to the test in her leadership capacity when a teacher alerted her about the negative impact of the actions of an upset student. The student took offense to the school's COVID-19 protection guidelines that requires everybody on campus to wear a mask and to complete a quick self-test before a class. He not only refused to comply, he also felt responsible for taking up the debate with other students about manipulation of the government and university and that this control would lead to the kinds of threats the Jewish populations were exposed to during Germany's Nazi regime. Berit Ann Roos knew she had to intervene. She wrote to the student, suggesting a meeting to discuss his concerns and asked him to stop mobilizing the students with his messages until the meeting. The student promptly wrote back, thanking her for the meeting suggestion and saying that unfortunately he could not – in good conscience – stop his mobilization, which he felt was critical to uphold. Berit Ann Roos cleared her calendar and arranged to see him at short notice in an attempt to contain the damage. Her assistant took part in the meeting, functioning also as study coach. As study coach, she was adamant about the rules and had little understanding or affinity for the position of the student, since she had become infected with COVID-19 herself during work at the academy. This happened despite all the safety measures the university had taken.

During the online meeting, Berit Ann Roos was composed, calm, and open to the perspective of the student. A close friend of hers had expressed doubts about being vaccinated and had outlined many perspectives of corona opponents. As a result, Berit Ann

DOI:10.4324/9781003305941-17

Roos brought a larger meta-level perspective to the table that would prove relevant. She listened carefully to the arguments that the student put on the table justifying his thinking and his behavior. The student pointed to the values of the university and asked her as a director to take a position with regard to welcoming everybody and not excluding anybody, regardless of their opinion. He also specifically asked her to share her personal opinion and not only her professional one. After thinking if her personal opinion would be relevant in this meeting, she told him that, personally, she did not feel particularly threatened or afraid of COVID-19. However, in her role as director of the academy, she had to assume a different position. As director, her job was to protect the school and all of its members to the best of her ability and this included setting up rules that were designed to protect the majority of the students and faculty. She asked him what it was he was afraid of. The student responded that he was truly afraid that he would not be able to continue to study architecture without giving up his values. After embracing his concern, she asked him to try to understand that: other students might feel the same intensity of fear, but the fear of being infected by COVID-19; that she felt responsible for *all* her students; and that his actions might cause other students to stay home out of fear. Her assistant then took the lead and explained how her infection with COVID-19 had impacted her life and that of her whole family. The emotions of the student and the assistant clashed and Berit Ann Roos intervened. She asked him kindly to wear a mask and to self-test in future so that other students would feel safe. The student responded: "Well, I don't see why this is my problem, I don't agree with your assessment and unfortunately I cannot act against my values." Berit Ann Roos took a slow breath and leaned back. She asked him: "Don't you think that your personal freedom stops where the freedom of another is impacted? Isn't that a basic rule of living together in our society?" He stared at her and then stared into the space behind her. His face changed. Berit Ann Roos has managed to stop his worried mind and to slow down his thinking. A space opened and they looked each other in the eyes.

Although Berit Ann Roos knew that she had to have him both wear a mask and to commit to self-tests, she needed to offer him a way out. She convinced him to wear a mask, and let the need to self-test slip by. She assumed that he would not be self-testing and knew this was a risk she took. She also knew that not all students complied with the self-testing and that forcing him would have broken the straw. After the meeting, her assistant exploded. She could not understand how patient Berit Ann Roos was with this student and why she did not argue harder for what she knew was right. She explained that while she knowingly abandoned the official rules and thereby created an officially accepted exception, to her this was about how to bridge two sides of an argument. Berit Ann Roos realized that she still felt calm and that this calmness was in all likelihood the deciding factor in how she managed to unblock a highly polarized situation with what to her was an acceptable, even a positive result.

A few days later, a second student wrote to her. He shared that he felt afraid to come to class because he was afraid to contract the virus. He had a newly born child at home and his girlfriend suffered from a rare disease. He felt he could not expose them by attending courses where not everything was done to prevent the spread of the virus. He asked her to enforce the self-testing rule, which had obviously been ignored by an increasing number of students.

As the initiator of the shared values of the architecture school, Berit Ann Roos instinctively knew what to do. In an engaged stakeholder process, these had been defined as "Act Consciously, Get Dirty, Add Value." She decided to write an email to all students and all faculty – something she rarely does.

Dear students

I want to share with you a matter that is close to my heart. This time, in which the Corona virus is still amongst us, is challenging for all of us and it is also accompanied with fear. The fear of getting infected with Corona, or infect loved ones, on the one hand, and the fear of losing the freedom of choice, on the other hand, may make it harder to understand each other, to learn with each other and to be with each other. The academy is a place where all of you are welcome, a place where different opinions are valued and a place of safety and community. This is only possible if we act consciously toward ourselves and others. With the prospect of better circumstances after the summer break, we have a few more weeks to go in which the ones that want to protect themselves with a vaccination don't have that possibility, yet. Therefore, I urgently ask all of you to be conscious of that fact and do everything in your power to not only protect yourself but all members of our learning community, the best you can! Only this way we can provide a safe environment and add value to our whole learning community.

I thank you very much for your effort until the summer and wish you many inspiring, warm, and happy moments with your fellow students and teachers, since we can finally meet each other again.

Kind regards
Berit Ann Roos

The email had a positive effect. She received no complaints from either student, as everybody appeared to understand that it was only together and by caring for the greater good that this current crisis could be overcome. Berit Ann Roos had managed the impossible: She had managed to unite highly polarized positions through a shared vision. She did so compassionately and with a calm and conscious demeanor. She herself was a role model for the values of the school. She did not flinch to get her hands dirty and she acted consciously through her ability to listen rather than judge.

This story summarizes the challenge of overcoming polarized conflicts. Berit Ann Roos was able to create a human connection by being able to create a distance to her own opinion and therefore being able to listen to her students with an open heart. Berit Ann Roos was able to step back from her own perspective, acknowledging both her personal views and her position given the role she held. In the end, the solution was anchored in the shared values they had developed together. She managed to create trust that enabled a pathway so that everybody agreed on a higher purpose and set aside their own positions sufficiently to dedicate their efforts to finding a solution for the shared common purpose they developed.

Insights from research

Trust is needed particularly in times of turbulence and volatility. Trust is the elixir that holds society together and creates a basis of common purpose and the ability to move forward together.

The Edelman Trust report suggests that every institution must play its part in restoring society and suggests that government leaders must lead with the courage to talk straight and address people's fear, acting with genuine empathy. It is critical for government leaders to argue using facts, providing trustworthy information that is truthful, unbiased, and reliable. Furthermore, all institutions should partner to solve urgent issues. As such, business, government, media, and NGOs must first find a common purpose and then find approaches to take collective action to address the burning issues of society.[1]

Nonetheless, more is needed to rebuild the trust in institutions. As long as social media players, such as Facebook, Twitter, TikTok, and YouTube, are not held liable for how their algorithms work, they will continue to favor those posts that are at the edge of what is permitted. The closer to the edge, the more it triggers users; and what these social media providers seek more than anything else is user engagement. Friendly posts do not generate engagement; eccentric, outrageous, suggestive posts attract attention and create engagement. Shockingly, 50% of users that joined an eccentric group did so on suggestion and prompting of a Facebook algorithm, Hany confirms. Social networks have a commercial interest in seeking out those posts and those actors that create most engagement, and hence support their ad-based business model that is built on an active and engaged audience. Hany suggests that there is a clear need for government regulations of the tech industry. All other attempts have not provided the change needed. He suggests that social media network players must be held liable for the damage they cause to prevent a further deterioration of trust in our institutions, governments, media, and science.

While the challenge lies indeed in system change that focuses on re-creating trust in our societal institutions, there is more to it than that. Nothing has polarized societies as much as the questions around COVID-19. In the United States, the pandemic is highly politized as the opposing Republican party is highly critical of all COVID-19 measures. The situation is heated and charged, and it creates pressure on democratic processes. Organizations also suffer from a significant disengagement or disenchantment of their employees, and there is so much at stake at the individual level.

In 2021, a record number of employees either quit their jobs or thought about doing so, a McKinsey study highlights.[2] In the United States, 40% of employees across all industries stated that they are almost certainly, very likely, likely, or somewhat likely to quit their jobs in the next three to six months. What is equally astonishing is that 36% of those who had quit their job in the past six months did so without having secured a new job. These employees express various levels of disenchantment with their organizations. The top factors employees cite as reasons for quitting are that they do not feel valued by their manager or their organization and that they did not feel a sense of belonging at work. The pandemic has irrevocably changed what people expect from work. Organizations are challenged to rethink how they make sense of their role in society both for themselves and as a means to remain an attractive employer.

On the individual level, research shows that the growing polarization is felt widely across society. In summer 2021, 62% of Swiss citizens had been involved in an argument about how to deal with the COVID-19 pandemic, with nearly half of those arguments in a close, personal environment, while 26% of respondents indicated that they have cut off contact with a personal relation due to divergent views.[3] This is concerning news. While individuals are challenged, often emotionally, in how to deal with divergent positions of people they care for, as a society we need to learn how to embrace this tension.

Katja Rost, sociologist at the University of Zurich, helps frame this need. She confirms that it is indeed the role of society to hold, to embrace, to accept this tension, and that society can do that.[4] Katja Rost suggests that a democratic society has implicitly agreed to struggle for answers rather than to stick to old answers without a process of questioning these when new insights emerge. This process of struggling for answers lies at the heart of an active democracy. The source of the current debate in society that causes such polarization lies in the tensions between the individual right for freedom from government and the collective rules and regulations that protect and serve the common good. This is a fight that humanity leads since its beginning. This fight for an answer is what differentiates humans from animals. We struggle and fight about topics as we advance with temporal solutions until these solutions need to be revised in a new struggle for answers.

With 64% of the global survey participants saying that people in their country lack the ability to have constructive and civil debates, we know that we have a serious problem at hand that needs solving. We need to find solutions to bridge the polarization that pulls our societies apart. With trust in government further declining, people have new and larger expectations for the role of business and NGOs. Across the globe, to varying degrees, government is considered largely as incompetent and unethical. Business, on the other hand, is considered as competent and NGOs are considered as ethical. People expect business and NGOs to step up and to provide societal leadership. Eighty-one percent of people surveyed demand that organizational leaders (CEOs) must be personally visible and engage on hot societal topics. The expectations of business are multi-sourced, with consumers, employees, and investors all expecting business to step up and to contribute positively to the societal challenges. The challenge consists of stepping up both as individuals and collectively as organizations.[5]

Recommendations

Working together with others is required as soon as an individual or an organization seeks to contribute to a larger project. Traditionally, organizations work with their clients and their suppliers in defined roles and with clearly determined objectives. It is about delivering a product or service delivered with the required quality and meeting all kinds of regulatory requirements and more along the way. Michael Porter's Five Forces model has portrayed this thinking since the late seventies. The Five Forces model shows the organization at the center with its traditional stakeholders grouped around it. When adopting an outside-in view, an organization reconsiders its place and realizes that it is but one of many stakeholders in society that is embedded in our natural environment. This outside-in perspective then allows a different engagement with other players resulting in true for-purpose co-creation.

The two mindset transformations that are required to embrace an outside-in perspective are about the individual challenge and the organizational challenge. At the individual level, the transformation relates to a capacity to overcome the "me" focus to embrace a "we" thinking; it is about being open rather than closed. At the organizational level it is about transforming from a competitive spirit to embracing co-creation; it is about seeing

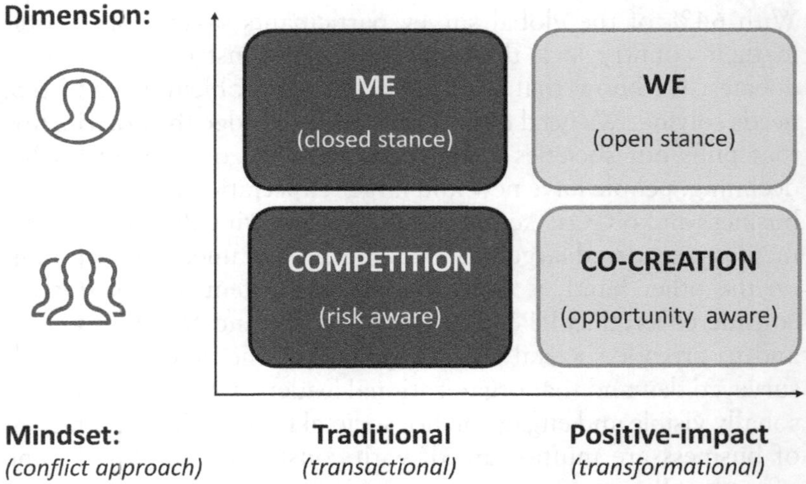

Figure 13.1 The individual and organizational mindset transformations

opportunities instead of risks (see Figure 13.1). The research into Positive Impact Organizations highlights that the two mindset transformations are predictors for an organizational change from a traditional inside-out perspective to a truly sustainable outside-in perspective. Once these mindsets are in place, it is only a question of time until the organization starts to deliver value for society and the planet.

There is more to it. If we consider how a society would have to transform, we need to take into account systemic factors and players, and for this a continuous strong democratic system is of prime importance. A strong democracy is something we can no longer take for granted as we have realized with the impact of the growing polarization and the impact of President Putin attempting to occupy the neighboring country the Ukraine. A reconsideration of how to strengthen our established rule of law and reinforce the global institutional agreements of how we treat conflict and human rights is clearly necessary. This is a topic that merits its own book and will require insights and experience beyond mine. In this book, I focus on the institutions that are able to operate within an existing functioning system, and such a system consists of organizations and of individuals. Both are capable of bringing about change in both classic and polarized situations. This is our focus here.

Individuals can change from a traditional me-focused mindset to a transformed we-oriented mindset by transforming from an ego-centric stance to an eco-centric stance. In other words, this means from having no access to what is going on inside themselves to becoming guided by inner values, which can be observed by a person no longer following what is fashionable but rather taking a stance for what is right. It can also be described as a transformation from being self-focused to prioritizing the needs of others, which often comes with an ability to let go of the convenient solution and to embrace a more principled position, even if it comes at personal cost. Organizations can change from a competitive mindset to a co-creation mindset by transforming from a competitive spirit to a co-creation spirit. This can be observed by the organization shifting from being focused primarily on its own internal priorities to agreeing on a purpose that is above and beyond its own direct interests. Along with it comes the increasing capacity to accept rather than reject differences of opinions in discussions and to recognize such differences as opportunities for growth. This can also be observed in how the organization deals with differing values: Are values in competition or is the organization able to see a benefit in values jointly developed with those stakeholders it needs to work with. As a result, there is a sense in the organization to be increasingly part of a larger movement far beyond its industry and a sense to be connected with a higher important purpose that serves society and ideally also the planet.

Notes

1 The 2021 Edelman Trust Barometer: www.edelman.com/trust/2021-trust-barometer
2 De Smet, A., Dowling, B., Mugayar-Baldocchi, M., and Schaninger, B. (2021): *'Great Attrition' or 'Great Attraction'? The Choice Is Yours.* McKinsey Quarterly. Accessed online August 28, 2022: https://www.mckinsey.com/business-functions/people-and-organizational-performance/our-insights/great-attrition-or-great-attraction-the-choice-is-yours
3 Flüglister, L. (2021): 60 Prozent hatten schon Streit wegen Umgang mit Corona. *SRG-Corona-Monitor*, July 23: www.srf.ch/news/schweiz/srg-corona-monitor-60-prozent-hatten-schon-streit-wegen-umgang-mit-corona?wt_mc_o=srf.share.app.srf-app.email
4 Widmer, B. (2021): Wieso sorgt die Pandemie für derart viele Konflikte? *SRG-Corona-Monitor*, July 23: www.srf.ch/news/schweiz/srg-corona-monitor-60-prozent-hatten-schon-streit-wegen-umgang-mit-corona?wt_mc_o=srf.share.app.srf-app.email
5 The 2022 Edelman Trust Barometer: www.edelman.com/trust/2022-trust-barometer

14 The individual positive impact mindset

Short story: a German actor experiences a shock therapy

Jan Josef Liefers is a well-known actor, musician, and film director in Germany. Since 2002, he has been starring in the highly popular crime series "Tatort," and he is somewhat of an influencer. In spring 2021, during the peak of the COVID-19 pandemic, he became involved in the protest opposing national pandemic measures. As part of an anti-government action involving 50 celebrities (#allesdichtmachen), he published an infamous video message that ridiculed the government measures. He closed his video message satirically with the saying "despair but don't doubt," suggesting that the measures were exaggerated and unnecessary.

The celebrity protest triggered a violent backlash. Other celebrities, doctors, and politicians voiced their disagreement. The anesthetist, Carola Holzner, also known as Doc Caro, called on the 50 celebrities to please form their own opinion before reaching such impossible conclusions. Jan Josef Liefers took her up on the offer and agreed to spend a day as an "intern" with her on the emergency unit for COVID-19 patients. He not only agreed to the experiment; he also decided to write about it, sharing how the experience had radically changed his position. He wrote that all COVID-19 patients in intensive care were seriously ill, closer to death than life. He also wrote that all of them were young, from 28 to 48 years old, and all were unvaccinated. He calls the experience a shock therapy that opened his eyes.

This story highlights the incredibly powerful impact of a lived experience. Since we are mostly surrounded by people with experiences similar to those we have, it is incredibly hard to put ourselves in other people's shoes. We cannot imagine what we do not experience. When Jan Josef Liefers accepted the internship

DOI:10.4324/9781003305941-18

invitation, it transformed him. The actor confirmed that he was no longer able to ignore what he had experienced and that he felt compelled to help others understand this new perspective.[1]

Much like a human connection, a lived experience provokes something real in a human being. This real sentiment or experience operates very differently from a mental input, such as a news item or a claim. Embodied experiences are anchored in our cells and remain much more vivid and present with us than a new mental input. In pedagogy, such an experience is called experiential learning; its effectiveness is significantly higher than listening to a lecture. Research suggests that experiential learning has a retention rate of 90% compared to a traditional lecture with a retention rate of 5% to 15%.[2]

When you search for manners to create a human connection with somebody you profoundly disagree with, why not spend time in their shoes alongside them to experience their perspective? They may be willing to step into your shoes, too, and you both would be a major step closer to finding a higher ground that can serve as a foundation to solve your disagreement.

Insights from research

Are there any specific methods to prepare for and support the mindset transformation from "me" to "we"? In Part III we highlighted the two different mindsets and what differentiates them. In this section, we investigate what the differentiators of a flexible mind are. A flexible mind is required to complete any kind of mindset transformation and therefore the foundation of training is the new muscle of an outside-in leadership mindset or a co-creative organization mindset.

What do we know from research about the capacity to be adaptive? Adaptability depends on flexibility. Adaptability is required in a continuously changing world and research shows that people with a strong psychological capital are best equipped for this adaptation.[3] German teacher and psychologist, Rüdiger Reinhardt, attributes four core competencies to a healthy psychological capital: confidence in the future, resilience, self-efficacy, and realistic optimism. In his career as a teacher and researcher, he developed pragmatic suggestions for strengthening each of them.

Confidence in the future is the capacity to think in alternative scenarios. It is not about having blind hope but rather the conviction that there are many means to reach a goal. Parallel prototyping is an ideal method to develop such alternative scenarios; it involves developing multiple solutions in quick feedback rounds that serve as a filtering process. The result is two-fold: a final solution that everybody involved understands, and the shared knowledge that there are also other pathways to achieve the same solution. This process is called way power; it is about the ability to successfully plan a path. Way power goes hand in hand with will power that is required to allocate a required energy to walk the initial or adapted paths.

Resilience is defined by the capacity to sustain and to recover. It is the quality of a bamboo tree that bends with the wind but does not break. A great manner to foster resilience is to reappraise a challenging situation and our reaction to it. Rüdiger Reinhardt suggests three steps to conduct such a reappraisal. First, to stop and then to inhale and exhale slowly and deeply three times. This activates the parasympathetic nerve system and quiets the mind. Second, to name the emotions you experience. It is proven that calling out the emotion we feel, measurably reduces our agitation. Third, to reassess the situation by asking what is positive about the event, and what can I learn from it for an inevitable next time? Such a new interpretation effectively dries up negative emotions. Reassessments focus on what is positive in any given situation.

Self-efficacy is about knowing that we can achieve something and being convinced that we are able to succeed when it matters. The more positive experiences we collect, the more mental proof we assemble. Self-efficacy is the realistic conviction that we are most likely successful in our endeavors. It is about gathering the courage to surpass a fear of failure and inner resistance. What others think about us influences how we think about ourselves. If others believe we can be successful, this has a positive effect on our own self-efficacy. Self-efficacy is increased when we have mastered a challenge and have overcome an obstacle. It is reflected in whether such successes, rather than failures, are top of our mind.

Realistic optimism is rational optimism; it is derived from a series of beliefs and competencies that help us focus on the positive aspect of life rather than the negative ones. Life consists only to a small percentage of what happens to you and to a dominating percentage of what you make out of it. And indeed, studies show that only 25% of an optimistic attitude is based on our gene pool. There is much room to develop an optimistic attitude.

If confidence in the future, resilience, self-efficacy, and realistic optimism are the core competencies of adaptability, it becomes clear that only a positive person can have a flexible mindset. It is all about reframing our experiences, about continuously reassessing and seeing the positive in what we experience, and developing the will power to stick to our journey, irrespective of what path opens up in front of us. It is also about surrounding ourselves with others who reinforce our self-belief and who support us in trusting that we will succeed.

And there is more to it. To be flexible in complex or chaotic times, it is of essence to acknowledge that we do not know it all and that we may have issues orienting ourselves. This is no easy task, as it is our natural instinct wanting to control the situation, particularly when it is falling out of control. My research fellow of the Leadership for Transition project, Anne Caspari, has realized that there is a need for alternative methods to handle such situations. Her work is based on research conducted by Dave Snowden, a researcher and consultant in the field of knowledge management and the application of complexity science.

Anne Caspari suggests that sensemaking allows structuring situations that are complex and unpredictable and that cannot be resolved with a plan or with previously established scenarios. Her research highlights that it is essential to initially come up with a plausible understanding of what is going on – and this is where sensemaking comes in. It involves testing ideas and assumptions through probing and sensing. Sensemaking focuses on micro interventions. These are based on the idea that culture is a process of finding meaning in the sum of daily interactions. Anne Caspari has learned that listening to micro stories of such interactions is a great manner of figuring out what goes on and for creating a space where participants of different backgrounds can together build a path forward.

The sense-making activity also allows mapping the disposition of people. Are they open or closed to change? If they are closed to change, an initial step involves finding out what might change their disposition so that they become more open. Sense-making work has identified that listening to unfamiliar stories can become a bridge from a closed to an open disposition. There is magic in sharing micro stories about small daily interactions; they can become transformative triggers. They also contribute to creating the human connection we have identified as critical in polarized situations where different participants may share contradicting micro stories.

Insights from research support our findings in practice that it takes a certain mental capacity – a flexibility of the mind – and an ability to engage in a human connection by sharing small personal stories and by listening to others sharing theirs. This may sound like nothing big or surprising. It is indeed very practical advice that anybody can build on. Find out where you become judgmental, and find mental flexibility within yourself to keep listening with an open heart. It will create a human connection that serves as a basis to let go of individual perspectives so that a higher purpose can be found which serves a higher cause that matters to everybody involved – and this is what the shift from "me" to "we" is all about.

Recommendations

We have learned that the creation of a human connection – ideally through dialogue – is a proven pathway to overcome polarized conflicts. We also know that not everybody is open or willing to create such a connection or to engage in a dialogue. We highlighted earlier how to help people shift from a closed to an open mind, suggesting that a certain flexibility of the mind exists. Particularly in polarized conflicts, this flexibility is short-lived. In this section, we are interested to explore manners to help opening the mind of those who may not be so easily convinced, for whatever reason, to connect to another person on a human basis.

We shall explore two steps: First, we need to convince the other person to sit down with us. Then, we need to convince the person to explore options that are acceptable to both and resolve the often-complex issue at hand. This relates both to classic and polarized conflicts, as the person we face is unlikely to bring the flexibility for the mindset transformation needed to resolve a complex polarized issue. We need a new approach. Let us see what can be done about this.

To begin, let us explore how we can convince a person who is unpersuadable to sit down with us to talk. Wharton business school professor, Adam Grant, has spent much time assessing how to change the mind of those considered unpersuadable.[4] He has studied individual corporate leaders, such as Steve Jobs, who are known for their stubbornness, arrogance, and narcissistic traits. Based on the growing evidence[5] that personality traits are not necessarily consistent from one situation to the next, he has identified approaches to open their minds. Adam Grant highlights that everybody has if/then triggers; a pattern of responding to particular scenarios in certain manners. He has identified four means to adjust these triggers for different outcomes:

1. **Adjusting arrogance:** The best manner for arrogant persons to be humbled is to have them explain something that is complex to describe. They will discover that they actually cannot fully explain what they thought they knew and this results in them pulling back their normal arrogance.
2. **Adjusting stubbornness:** Success and failure are determined by external or internal factors. Stubborn people tend to believe in internal control; they think that outcomes can be determined by their will. Do not try to convince such a person with external arguments; they believe that their outcomes are controlled solely by them. Do involve them in the shaping of new solutions, let them come up with their own ideas by planting seeds that they can pick up and consider as their own. Research shows that asking questions instead of giving answers helps overcome people's defensiveness.[6] Questions such as "What if?" and "Could we?" spark creativity by making people curious about what is possible.
3. **Adjusting narcissism:** Do not tell a narcissist that they are wrong; they do not appreciate it, as they believe themselves to be superior and special. It takes a careful framing to coax

them into acknowledging that they are flawed and fallible. Research suggests that narcissists suffer from an unstable self-esteem.[7] Since narcissists crave status and approval, they tend to become hostile when they feel insulted, rejected, or shamed. The approach to have them change their minds is to appeal to their desire to be admired. This is best done by praising them in an area different from the one in which you hope to change their minds. If you think they made a wrong decision, do not compliment them on their decision-making capacity; rather compliment their creativity or any other positive trait or competency they have. We all have multiple identities. When we feel secure about one of our strengths, we become more open to accepting our shortcomings elsewhere.[8]

4. **Adjusting disagreeableness**: In contrast to these pathways, people who are argumentative require a different approach. It is important to stand up to them rather than back down. Argumentative persons tend to view people with different opinions as competitors, demanding a different strategy. Disagreeable people are energized by conflict and as a result they interpret bending to their will as a weakness. Stay your ground and gain their respect.

Once the previously unpersuadable person has shifted to a more neutral mental state, we can envision solving the conflict at hand. This brings us to step two: developing solutions with a person who finds it challenging to step beyond the conflict at hand. I have compiled this list based on research conducted by psychology journalist, Rebecca Webber.[9] The five suggestions can be used with people who may not bring the required flexibility of the mind to shift toward a positive impact mindset.

1. **Accept the starting point**: Former deputy campaign manager for Barack Obama, Stephanie Cutter, has learned what it takes to resolve conflicts with others. She suggests that you have to understand people's situations and where they come from – and start from where they are and not from where you would like them to be. This is fundamental advice that should be used at the start of meeting with anybody irrespective of what we attempt to achieve together.
2. **Ask open-ended questions**: Negotiation coach, Lisa Gates, suggests to approach somebody who holds a different

opinion than us by taking a step back and asking them open-ended questions about their preference or point of view. Approach it with an open mind as if you would conduct an interview. Learning from them what is important to them may help you discover how you both can achieve what you want. This approach works particularly well in classic conflicts where win-win solutions work.

3. **Reframe the conversation:** Howard Gardner, professor at the Harvard Graduate School of Education, suggests that we cannot address fear directly, but that the only thing we have to fear is fear itself. Try to find a means to recast the topic you disagree about so that the other person is prompted to think about things differently. This reframing may lead you to create a long-term impact on how the other person thinks about her or his position.[10] This is a great approach in a polarized conflict situation, as it may lead to a new, higher perspective.
4. **Show the holes in your argument:** Journalist Megan McArdle advises that instead of giving the other person only the points that make your case, be up front about the drawbacks of your argument and address them. In doing so, you show that you understand the complexity of the situation and that you are honest. Addressing the whole spectrum of the point of discussion makes you more trustworthy and therefore easier to listen to.[11] This is an excellent point of advice to gain trust and a human connection to then explore a shared purpose together.
5. **Be sympathetic**: Psychologist Robert Cialdini highlights the importance of being sympathetic and benevolent to the other person.[12] He suggests to always think the very best of the other. People like it when they are liked. And they will want to return this benevolence. A positive relationship is the very foundation of being able to listen and to potentially embrace a deep change in oneself.

May these recommendations be of help when you need to collaborate with a person who holds a different opinion to yours and is unwilling or unable to engage in the recommended approach to overcome polarized conflicts, developed in the book and summarized in the previous chapter. We know what works: first re-creating a human connection and then engaging in a dialogue to discuss the two realities you both bring to the table to explore a new dimension that includes both your realities and embraces a higher shared vision. This takes a "we" mindset and enables co-creative solutions. And yet, not everybody's mind brings that flexibility to embrace such a positive impact leadership mindset.

Notes

1 Thomas, F. (2021): Auf der Intensivstation die Meinung geändert. *Tages-Anzeiger*, October 10.

2 Prussia, G.E., and Weis, W.L. (2004): Experiential learning effects on retention: Results from a required MBA course. *Journal of College Student Retention: Research, Theory & Practice*, 5(4), 397–407: https://doi.org/10.2190/5NU3-FCP6-LU88-5282

3 Reinhardt, R. (2013): *Psychologisches Kapital – Durch Nutzung psychischer Ressourcen zu höherer Führungseffektivität*. Hamburg: Windmühle Verlag.

4 Grant, A. (2021): *Think Again: The Power of Knowing What You Don't Know*. New York: Viking.

5 Walter Mischel, W., Shoda, Y., and Mendoza-Denton, R. (2002): Situation-behavior – profiles as a locus of consistency in personality. *Current Directions in Psychological Science*, 11(2), 50–54: https://doi.org/10.1111/1467-8721.00166

6 Sprott, D.E., Spangenberg, E.R., Block, L.G., Fitzsimons G.J., Morwitz, V.G., and Williams, P. (2006): The question – behavior effect: What we know and where we go from here. *Social Influence*, 1(2): https://doi.org/10.1080/15534510600685409

7 Baumeister, R.F., Bushman, B.J., and Campbell, W.K. (2000): Self-esteem, narcissism, and aggression: Does violence result from low self-esteem or from threatened egotism? *Current Directions in Psychological Science*, 9(1), 26–29: https://doi.org/10.1111/1467-8721.00053

8 Geoffrey, L., Cohen, G.L., and Sherman, D.K. (2014): The psychology of change: Self-affirmation and social psychological intervention. *Annual Review of Psychology*, 65, 333–371: https://doi.org/10.1146/annurev-psych-010213-115137

9 Webber, R. (2014): Five ways to change someone's mind: www.realsimple.com/work-life/life-strategies/change-someones-mind

10 Gardner, H. (2006): *Changing Minds*. Boston, MA: Harvard Business Review Press.

11 McArdle, M. (2015): *The Upside of Down: Why Failing Well Is the Key to Success*. New York: Penguin Publishing Group.

12 Cialdini, R. (2007): *Influence – The Psychology of Persuasion*. New York: Harper Collins Publishing.

15 The organizational positive impact mindset

Short story: a Swiss CEO reports on the mounting pressure

Joost Sutter, at the time CEO of leading food retailer COOP, is a rare corporate leader in the Swiss business landscape. He is both successful and admired. He cares for the environment and considers the role of his organization to contribute positively to society. I had the opportunity to participate in an interview conducted by a journalist of the economic journal, *Bilanz*, for an article[1] for which I had contributed the methodology.

When asked about what he considers levers of change to influence those CEOs who do not yet consider sustainability as a corporate responsibility, Joost Sutter is pragmatic. He suggests that if a person does not understand it, there is little to do to change that. In his opinion, the external pressure on corporations is by now so large that a CEO can no longer ignore it. Consumers, civil society, the next generation – they all have significantly influenced how the role of business in society is perceived. In this decade, business is simply expected to do good, he says. The challenge for a CEO is how to do well while doing good, meaning how to keep up the financial performance while addressing the new demands of consumers and stakeholders. When pushing for more insights on how to persuade more CEOs to understand this, he suggests that the change from a simple profit focus to contributing positively to societal and environmental challenges is a change like any other. A CEO needs to go through the different stages of change. First, there is shock, then denial. Eventually, denial turns into a kind of a depressed state of acceptance from which emerges a new normal accompanied by a more positive sentiment.

To Joost Sutter, there is little sense in attempting to change somebody's mind. The intrinsic motivation belongs to the person and her or his preference, and is as complex as personal values. The

DOI:10.4324/9781003305941-19

only approach – according to him – lies in changing the extrinsic motivation. In case of the organizational mindset transformation, this occurs currently through the high external pressure of investors and shareholders. Changing the extrinsic motivation works; he has no doubt. Ultimately, CEOs will want to keep their job, and if the requirements for success change, they will simply realign to perform against these new standards. Joost Sutter is confident that the tipping point for business to care about more than just their financial performance has been reached owing to a cumulation of external pressures coming from civil society, their own children, and the investors. He points out that there is simply a new reality in which we operate and where the negative consequences of issues such as climate change are increasingly visible.

Joost Sutter takes the position that one cannot change the mind of somebody else. And yet, we have seen that there are avenues to explore. These involve creating a space where people with divergent views can meet and listen to each other with open ears and ideally open hearts. Once a person has an open mind, it is possible to envision change. Yet, if a person remains unpersuadable and closed minded, it is absolutely not possible to change their mind. From that perspective, Sutter is right.

It is possible, however, to participate in an exchange where both parties may emerge somewhat changed. This is reflected in Otto Scharmer's saying: "Nobody has come out of a good conversation unscathed." While maybe ironic, there is a deep truth to it. The short story about the Swedish city Eskilstuna in Chapter 12 shows that citizens and the government can both undergo deep change to their behavior and their expectations toward each other. It is a promising example for such change to happen. The story in Chapter 8 about how a Swiss city government has involved its members in a purpose-oriented innovation process that was based on enabling a trusting and open conversation about the future of the city demonstrates further how the exposure to new and different ideas not only opens the mind but also broadens the perspective of those involved.

Insights from research

Let us turn to insights from research to learn more about developing the right kind of organizational mindset. William

Isaacs, co-founder of the Organizational Learning Center at MIT's Sloan School of Management, has dedicated much of his life to understanding organizational change. He has developed a method called dialogic leadership. Dialogue, for him, is about holding meaningful conversations. William Isaacs calls it the art of talking and thinking together. Dialogue is extremely useful for creating solutions to wicked problems. Dialogue facilitators seek to create a space where the source of thinking becomes evident behind the words. It involves a process of shared listening with the purpose of hearing unanticipated possibilities. It reminds us of the importance of creating a human connection to overcome polarized conflict at the individual level.

One of the constraints of dialogue is that people may react with well-worn thought habits as they attempt to listen and rather than creating new solutions, parties become stuck in rigid, dug-in positions. William Isaacs points out that when the stakes are high the familiar routines are more likely to come out. Yet, true dialogue seeks to break out of this autopilot status so that participants can move beyond collaboration to achieve co-creation where they think and create together. To reach that stage, Isaacs has concrete recommendations for organizations interested to develop a co-creation capacity[2]:

1. **Create safe environments,** where it is possible to openly speak and think together. Most organizational cultures do not permit this and are rigidly set to avoid errors or to admit uncertainty or doubt.
2. **Build alignment for the true potential** instead of simply accepting what appears possible. Dare to envision new partnerships and collaborations to create the new rather than just reacting to the existing.
3. **Encourage personal awareness** how internal thoughts and actions impact the world around your organization. Learn to work with the invisible: What goes on with each of you, impacts what goes on out there with other stakeholders.
4. **Train your organizational change muscle.** Explore how your organizational memory and habits can be rewired so that the organization can act on the change that is reflected by realizing the true potential out there.

5. **Shift from thinking to acting to being.** Insights are great; however, a new manner of organizational leadership involves creating new attitudes, thoughts, and action. Find approaches to encourage members of your organization to implement concrete new behaviors and rituals that support the shared purpose on a daily basis.

These five suggestions are addressed so that forward-looking organizational leaders can find approaches across departments and regions to develop the co-creation muscle in the organization. The ultimate challenge is to enable not only members of the organizations and the organizational structure but also decision-making processes to empower and encourage a collaboration with external third parties with equal fluency as internally across departments.

When studying the diversity of organizational members, it is interesting to explore who might be most suited for such a change. William Isaacs has found out that there is a need for diverse personalities in any conversation. It takes more than just one type of person to develop a co-creation spirit in an organization. William Isaac offers an interesting four-player model. The model describes four players with different roles: the movers, the followers, the opposers, and the bystanders. He points out that it takes all four types to make progress. Movers initiate ideas; without them there is no direction. Followers complete what is said and support what is happening; without them there is no completion. Opposers challenge what is being said; without them there is no correction. Bystanders comment on what is happening; without them there is no perspective. This four-player model summarizes the important central dimension of dialogue. It is all about a particular balance between positions people advocate, and their willingness to step back and inquire about their own view and that of others. In the vast majority of conversations, advocacy is the only operating mode, and people hardly listen to what is said. These resemble more serial monologues and have little in common with a dialogue.

Recommendations

An organization may be defined as the sum of the individuals it consists of. While an organizational mindset is not the sum of the mindset of all members of the organization, it can be tilted when a certain number of individuals have transformed their mindset. Therefore, it is interesting to search for connectors between the individual and the organizational mindset to create positive impact. To illustrate this, let us consider realistic optimism, a core competency to develop a flexibility that is required for an open mind highlighted in Part IV. This individual competency is equally important for the organizational mindset. Let us consider a pragmatic exercise to increase realistic optimism: the grateful three. It is an optimism hygiene practice that works for individuals and teams. Here is how it works. Take two minutes at the end of each day and reflect on the day. Ask yourself or ask each team member: "What are three things you are grateful for?" and note them down. Ensure that the members of a team do not pick the same standard responses such as "my family, my health, my colleagues" but highlight what happened that particular day. Research suggests that noting down these points for a period of 21 days will result in lasting change. This exercise is an example of many such tools that help train both the individual as well as the organizational mindset muscle for positive impact.

The outside-in leadership mindset and the co-creative organizational mindset both focus on what is going on out there instead of observing the world from an inside-out perspective. It starts with focusing on the real-world problems and then considers what an individual or an organization can do about it. In times of conflict, this connection to the larger system, to society, and to nature may be lost. Social scientist, Brené Brown, is confident, however, that this connection can be found again. She points out that while belonging to each other cannot be denied, it can be truly lost.[3] We have learned that much of the efforts of bringing people with different perspectives together is about re-creating this connection. For individuals, we have focused on the flexibility of the mind. In this organizational section, we would like to recommend time-proven suggestions on how to help build the bridge between different parties. Charles Camosi of the Fordham University has carved out four practices his research suggests can help create such a connection again:[4]

1. **Speak from humility.** Recognizing that we are finite, flawed beings that are prone to making serious mistakes can help create such humility in ourselves. Remembering our flaws

and embracing this humility is of great help when somebody challenges our point of view. Humility is also important to create space in ourselves and others to changing our minds and to acknowledge flaws in our perspectives or arguments. There is no need to be flawless or perfect; let go of such ambition and be realistic with yourself and those around you.

2. **Work on a strong partnership.** Developing a solid partnership involves active listening with the intent of finding something to learn. This includes sharing personal stories and things we care about. It also involves actually responding to what is being said, sticking to the topic discussed – and it may require an effort to acknowledge our own biases about gender, race, level of privilege, or sexual orientation that may stand in our path to listen openly.
3. **Avoid binary thinking.** Most issues of our times, and in particular the issues multistakeholders meet about, are too complex to fit into simplistic black-or-white categories. Focus on responding always with "and" rather than "but." Your perspective enriches the other as much as theirs enriches yours. Avoid categorizing in your mind so that you can engage seriously and in an open manner.
4. **Use constructive language.** Do actively monitor what you say and self-censor the use of dismissive words. There is nothing wrong with apologizing if your mouth is quicker than your brain. Remember, you want to engage the others in the room into a fruitful exchange of ideas. This requires a respectful tone and use of words.

The many grassroot initiatives that are created by engaged citizens are excellent examples of how these recommendations work in practice. In Austria, for example, there are online round tables "For-a-New-Being-Together," which has emerged as a result of the polarized positions during the COVID-19 pandemic (https://coronaaussoehnung.org). The project has been launched with the desire to create an open space for considering additional aspects and perspectives regarding the COVID-19 crisis. Its objective is to find an approach to overcome the growing polarization caused by the very divergent views of how to resolve the crisis. The project illustrates very nicely the best practice insights and recommendations we have developed.

It is important to point out that we often underestimate to what degree challenging conversations involve body language and attitude. Psychologist Kevin Dutton suggests keeping your message short and simple, focusing on the benefits to the other person, and surprising them with something odd. He suggests being very confident and look the person in the eye, nod when they nod, and be empathic.[5] These are suggestions that are framed in a classic conflict setting, yet body language and attitude are just as important in a polarized conflict. There, an authentic focus and attention on the human connection will be key for progress.

Last but not least, let us also remember that we live in a global village with many different cultures and social practices present. Insights on body language and other types of interpersonal engagement may not work equally well across all cultures and societies. Indian-born American, Deepak Chopra, refers to certain universal truths when collaborating with others. He highlights the importance to be sincere and truthful, meaning that it is important not to manipulate others. He suggests that when you understand the other person's or organization's belief system, build on it and appeal to what they believe. Deepak Chopra suggests being careful with assumptions on the other, including the assumption that the other person is open-minded. He finds that it is helpful to see the blind spots of the other party so that you do not step into them. Do not make the other person feel wrong; make them feel right. Last but not least, he makes an important point: A conversation is always a combination of reason and emotion; probably more of the former than the latter. Be emotionally aware, of your emotions and also of the emotions of those across from you.

Notes

1 Kuhn-Spogat, I. (2021): Green-running. CEOs vor! Das «Green Business CEO»-Rating bewertet erstmals nicht nur Facts &Figures zur Nachhaltigkeit, sondern stellt die CEOs ins Rampenlicht. *Bilanz Zeitschrift*, June 30: www.handelszeitung.ch/bilanz/green-running

2 Isaacs, W. (2021): Accessing genuine dialogue. *The Watercooler – Straight Talk on Strategic Issues*, 6(4), July/August 2012, 9–11: www.watercoolernewsletter.com

3 Brown, B. (2017): *Braving the Wilderness*. New York: Ebury Publishing.

4 Jackson Rainer, J. (2019): Five ways to have a civil conversation in a polarized society. *Next Avenue*, February 9, 2019.

5 Dutton, K. (2011): *Split-Second Persuasion: The Ancient Art & New Science of Changing Minds*. Boston, MA: Houghton Mifflin.

16 Working together for a better world

The mindset for collaborating in a complex world

We are in midst of the collective experience that uncertainty and complexity are here to stay. There is the IPPC report outlining the size of the climate crisis; the global COVID-19 pandemic; the Russian invasion of the Ukraine, which shatters our trust in the rule of law, forces the integration of refugees into our life, triggered the mobilization of the defense budgets, contributed to the break-down of the global supply chains, highlighted issues with the energy supply and dependencies with autocratic countries. The list is long. All of these elements point in one direction – we need to adapt our thinking and acknowledge that we are in a changed world context. The idea of sitting out a current crisis so that we can return back to normal has disappeared. Our sense of comfort has gone and is replaced by an uncertain and complex new reality. In such an uncertain and complex world, it takes a positive impact mindset to work together on new solutions.

In this context it means solutions that will not only have to solve the issues of the parties engaged in the solution but also contribute to a larger and more complex reality. A local government can no longer meet with local business to solve a current environmental, economic, or social issue. The parties will need to ensure that their solution also makes sense in the larger changing legislative framework and geopolitical development of surrounding nations. There is no longer a national energy, food, or refugee crisis; all of these issues are part of a larger and more complex transnational crisis. The ability to step beyond the traditional win-win mindset and to recognize and work toward the overarching issue requires a positive impact mindset. The mindset is defined by the ability to see beyond egoistic needs

DOI:10.4324/9781003305941-20

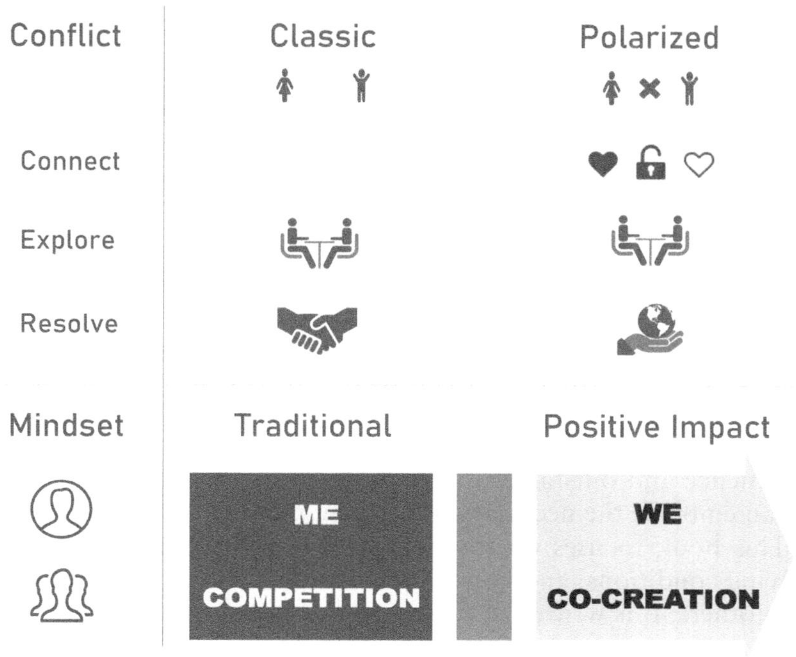

Figure 16.1 Summative overview of conflicts and mindsets

and, in a co-creative spirit, to embrace broader needs beyond our own interests in a spirit of co-creation and collaboration. Such a mindset is helpful in working out solutions in our complex world, and it is helpful in addressing the likely polarized conflicts that emerge along the way (see Figure 16.1).

Much research has gone into how to best work together to solve such overarching issues. I have been part of a team that has tested the Collaboratory methodology across Europe. For the past eight years, the Leadership for Transition team has worked on the challenge of multistakeholder groups working on societal issues. Initially, the Collaboratory methodology was developed in the context of the RIO+20 Conference in Rio de Janeiro in 2012, intended as a new methodology to help business schools redefine their role in society. The methodology is a potpourri of best practice methods in creating effective spaces for co-creation among conflicted multistakeholders. We have observed that it is an effective method for issue-centered one-day workshops, hosting people who have never met and who share a stake in a matter they are concerned with. The method is described in detail in the Collaboratory[1] book.

The original Collaboratory does not offer pathways for the follow-on implementation journey that follow such a one-day multistakeholder event. As we have observed in the Swedish Hospital case in Chapter 2, change does not happen in one session; it often takes tailor-made, adaptive, and well-facilitated spaces that enable participants to reach new solutions together. The "Five Superpowers for Co-creators" book served this purpose, outlining building blocks for a longer transformational process and highlighting the challenges during the process.[2] It has been successfully applied in the Swiss PRISMA case described in Chapter 6. We have also learned that it takes great patience and outstanding facilitation skills so that participants can embrace the necessary underlying mindset transformations. This book focuses on the mindset transformation, the underlying conditions, and how we can enable them in ourselves and in others. It is written in the context of polarized conflicts.

In view of our complex and polarized times, the definition of the Collaboratory has been broadened to include issues that fall into the responsibility of government. The development of future-oriented legislation requires an active collaboration of multiple players that have not traditionally worked together. Government is challenged to work outside of its political boundaries. There is a new role for business in contributing to government attempts to define appropriate legislation. This role is far different from the traditional lobbying attempts. Businesses that have been a part of Collaboratories have experienced the benefits of multistakeholder collaboration across sectors and have overcome the resistance to sit down with others that hold different worldviews and priorities. Governments have learned that they cannot create relevant legislation in a vacuum. They must collaborate with those that will be affected and integrate the perspective of pioneering organizations that demonstrate that entirely new pathways can work.

This type of multistakeholder collaboration is mostly new and represents an uncertain ground for many organizations and individuals involved. It is no surprise that such collaboration triggers varying degrees of concern or fear among participants, even more so in the context of polarization. This is where an awareness of the different mindsets and the different types of conflicts comes into play. It is helpful to concerned leaders and change agents, and it represents essential knowledge for multistakeholder facilitators.

We have explored the ins and outs of the ideal positive impact mindset and what it takes to embrace a transformation to embody it. Mindsets are not stable states. In favorable conditions, it may be quite easy to embrace a positive impact mindset. At other times, it may be just impossible to gather the strength for stepping beyond our own perspective and reach above and beyond our own needs. These are the interesting moments where learning comes in. When we experience things that confirm our bias, little to no learning happens. When, however, we face situations that contradicts our bias, the resulting resistance within ourselves is an excellent master for learning. This book serves to understand the friction of such moments and seeks to provide pathways forward. It is all about training the positive impact muscle one challenging moment at a time.

In the context of weakened democracies, training this muscle is of essence. Democracies build on the capacity of reaching a shared agreement, with debate and dialogue representing essential elements of finding such agreement. Polarized conflicts have highlighted the lack of a shared knowledge generation and truth finding. We are in a world that lacks a foundation for discussion. Different parties live in distinctly separate realities that are sourced from different information channels. The trust in media is at an all-time low. Social media favors extreme positions that create an emotional response, resulting in a significant distortion of the truth.

Seeing value in a shared truth is essential. We have explored the importance of creating a human connection to be able to open up to the other person and their perspective as a starting basis for a conversation. American journalist Jonathan Rauch suggests two basic laws in conversations that seek a shared knowledge and truth. First, nobody has the self-styled last word. This is based on the shared understanding that every insight is of a temporary nature and is only valid for as long it holds up to verification. If an insight cannot be verified, nobody – no authority, no activist – can close, stop, predetermine, or cancel a debate. Second, there is no personal authority. Every statement must be able to be verified by anybody. Nobody can establish a thesis, nobody has a free ticket to express the truth, irrespective of who they are and to what group they belong. Jonathan Rauch suggests that these two rules circumvent rhetoric maneuvers in debates.[3] We have learned of the limitations of debates and that these do not contribute to a mindset transformation. Yet, debates are a basic instrument of democracies; it is in everybody's interest to invest in our democracies and in the rule of law to operate as an agreed-upon framework for solving our global conflicts. In a complex and uncertain world, it will be essential to not only navigate the troubled waters of debate and democracy but to also learn to differentiate classic and polarized conflicts and to reflect on what mindset is at play both on our side and on the side of those we work with.

The facilitation challenges

Facilitators play a critical role in enabling future-relevant solutions that require multistakeholders to collaborate. When conflicts emerge, they often assume a mediation role, too. While many are trained in handling classic conflicts, there is a need for awareness in how to deal with polarized conflicts. As we notice an increase in cross-sector collaboration, more and more well-used democratic processes find their way into multistakeholder processes – and suddenly there are new participants in government processes.

Polarized conflicts require a different approach than classic conflicts. While debates are a much-used tool to understand a problem, they do not work in case of a polarized conflict. Dialogues work well in polarized conflicts, as the dialogues provide all parties the required space and time to express their perspectives, which is an important starting point in such situations.

Classic conflicts can be resolved by identifying a solution that works for all involved parties, a win-win solution. Polarized conflicts, on the other hand, first require that the involved parties agree on a common reality. To achieve that, a human connection must be built to create a foundation of respect. Characteristically, a shared reality is a third reality that emerges by having outlined the two opposing realities of the parties at conflict. This third reality represents a higher perspective or a shared vision that provides a larger benefit beyond serving the two conflicted parties. Polarized solutions are not win-win solutions; they are solutions that often serve the common good and that also satisfy the concerns of the involved parties. Achieving polarized solutions requires a transformational approach, whereas win-win solutions are usually purely of transactional nature.

Thankfully, not all multistakeholder processes originate with a conflict. In many cases, however, the conflicts emerge only over time, once stakeholders with different perspectives start working together. A facilitator will need to be able to read the signs and to adapt the process with the right method to ensure a results-oriented process.

Facilitating multistakeholder co-creation events includes an onboarding process with key stakeholders to ensure that their needs and expectations are clarified in the context of the project's vision. Such onboarding needs to happen ahead of a first stakeholder meeting, which serves to start building a foundation of trust among stakeholders. During the innovation process, the facilitator will have to manage the different levels of interaction among individuals, among groups, and at the larger issue level. There are challenges at each of these three levels, which can turn into potential showstoppers and need to be handled with great care.

In my book on the five superpowers, I have highlighted the key challenges of classic conflicts at the individual, the collective, and the overarching issue level. In classic conflict situations two opposing parties operate in a shared reality, which makes a potential solution much easier than in a polarized situation. There is one common insight that can be applied across all three types of challenges. When two parties disagree, each of them typically expresses a valid concern that is derived from a particular strength they possess. The strength simply becomes overstretched due to the other party insisting on an opposing view. Both parties overstretch their strengths to ensure that they are heard and this results in the underlying strengths being perceived as limitations. It is relatively easy to highlight the valid point in both views and to associate them to the original core strength. The trick suggested in the book on the five superpowers is to have the two parties identify the overarching superpower that combines the two strengths. Once such a superpower is found, both parties are re-engaged and on board to collaborate again. Both have been taken seriously and both have contributed to actively advancing the project due to their concern – an important trust-building experience for everybody involved.

A facilitator will also need to recognize when their own internal reaction is triggered and when it could stand in the way of a workshop progressing. The ability to differentiate between what is happening with others out there and what is being triggered here within me requires an ability to correctly sense and interpret the energies in the room and within oneself. This requires not only practice, but also supervision and introspection. Ongoing personal development to develop and refine this sensory capacity is part of a facilitator's ongoing practice. These different levels of diagnosis and differentiation serve so that a facilitator can indeed create and hold a space with the purpose of the multistakeholders engaged progressing toward resolving the agreed project vision.

When meetings fail, facilitators will first and foremost need to investigate their own stance during critical moments of the meeting. Did their own subconscious reaction stand in the way of the parties progressing? Facilitators pay great attention to this phenomenon called "standing in the way." It is the opposite of "creating and holding a space." There are easy and pragmatic manners to get "out of the way." For one, facilitators themselves often recognize that they are standing in the way of progress and they recognize how to maneuver out of troubled waters. And yet, a facilitator may feel overwhelmed and may not be able to see an immediate solution to step aside. In such a situation, there is no shame in suggesting to pause the session proceedings and to call for a break. A facilitator may, however, be at a loss of what to do and yet not want to call for a break not to lose the flow. In such a situation, it may make sense to transparently share what is happening, and that the facilitator is unclear if this is a personal reaction or if there is something in the room that needs to be addressed. Asking participants to sense if there is a resonance with what the facilitator perceives can help clarify things. If the facilitator has a sense of what may cause a blockage, she or he may choose to work with the issue to highlight an overarching problem that may occur at the meta-level, lifting the stakeholder focus from the dispute to a higher level. The facilitator may ask participants if this situation resembles by any means what might also be happening outside of the room. If the answer is affirmative, a facilitator may suggest tackling the situation pro-actively together. When participants experience that there is a pathway to progress even when things do not go as planned, this builds trust. Such an experience can set a positive precedence for everybody involved.

In my experience, it is incredibly liberating to admit such moments of feeling stuck. A facilitator is dependent to be in possession of a maximum amount of energy resources; a moment of uncertainty can drop these resources significantly. And yet, sharing transparently what is going on, liberates stuck energies and brings the resources back in in their entirety – and that is when facilitation is conducted in the best manner.

How can a facilitator assess the flexibility of a participant's mind? It may be quite relevant to estimate how far a person is able to stretch toward a positive impact mindset. One of the shortcuts is to assess a person's capacity to reason. Reasoning is developed as human beings mature into adults and it can be illustrated in how a people evolve in their essay-writing capacity. As young adults, we write essays that only use evidence that supports our own arguments. As we grow older, we start including evidence that weakens the opposing perspective, which we reject. And eventually, as we mature, we learn to add evidence to our story that is inconsistent with our position. We integrate arguments that weaken our position or support an opposing position. We have shifted from a black-and-white thinking to a capacity to notice nuances and shades. The capacity of an adult for argument-based reasoning is of critical importance when we use dialogue as a method of stakeholder engagement. Such reasoning is a necessary foundation for thinking in complex manners about a topic we care about; it not only involves including external arguments but also requires a capacity for introspection so that we can explore suppressed inner dissonances. In a dialogue setting, a person may start reflecting about a subconscious resonance that was triggered during an argument.[4] Such a reflection may provide a personal insight into why a person reacted how she or he did. The capacity to integrate both inner and outer contradictions to how we consider the world will make a dialogue a powerful tool.

Often, not all participants of a dialogue session have this capacity to reason, and it is up to the facilitator to create a space where everybody has their place and is heard. Clearly, there are also limits to a mindset transformation. There are world leaders that offer sad examples of how incapable they are to reason as adults or how to engage in any degree of introspection. Unfortunately, human development is not compulsory in life; it requires nurturing along the way. We may have to distance ourselves from people with a low developmental level or we need to acknowledge that it is highly unlikely to resolve a polarized conflict with them. Dialogue is not a solution to every problem as we explored in the previous chapter's recommendations.

Given the size of the challenge of such facilitation, it may well make sense to conduct such facilitation only as a team. Two persons will do a much better job creating and holding a space than one single person. Particularly in complex situations, it is of great help to have two facilitators at hand, one engaged in driving the discussion forward and the other focused on sensing what is happening in the room from an energetic perspective, including the emotions and non-verbal expressions of participants. It is, after all, the central responsibility of facilitators to provide the right tools and methods to ensure that the process leads to the right outcome within an agreed-upon time frame. This is called a process responsibility. Importantly, facilitators are not responsible for the content result, meaning the substance of the particular solution developed and proposed by the participants – this is the joint responsibility of all participating stakeholders. This difference is part of the ground rules a facilitator will set out at the start of each session, together with a formal agreement among all participants to respect the current non-competitive compliance laws in the jurisdiction of the event, as well as other important agreements regarding confidentiality, conflict of interest, and communication.

Concluding thoughts for leaders and change agents

Increasingly, pioneering individuals and organizations reach out to work together to create positive impact. For this to happen, a carefully crafted independent facilitation is clearly recommended. Change makers sometimes think they themselves can facilitate. This has proven counterproductive to their intent. When a person wants to defend both their own perspective and also serve as a facilitator, trust quickly evaporates. I recommend that as a leader, you insist on an external third-party facilitator, irrespective if you initiate or simply participate in a multistakeholder dialogue.

As a participant of a multistakeholder process, it all boils down to your ability to embrace opinions that are not your own. This is the co-creative muscle you need to train so that you can create positive impact. This takes courage, and research shows that it works. Talking to people who think differently will force you to open your mind. Inspired by the contact theory that has been developed to overcome tensions in racial and ethnic encounters, social psychologists, Tom Pettigrew and Linda Troop, analyzed the effectiveness of contact with people who think differently. Their meta-analysis featuring more than 700 independent sample studies suggests that prejudice is reduced by talking to people with different opinions.[5] There is hope. We must force ourselves to be more open than we are comfortable with.

Surveys in the United States and in Europe indicate that editors of quality press outlets have a tendency to be oriented to the left. This is not good news. We need divergent opinions, not the same reinforced opinions. Tom Rosenstiel, until recently the head of the American Press Institute, highlights that editorial teams must argue about different positions. Everybody agreeing is a sign of a dysfunctional team. Media may be distrusted because, increasingly, editorial teams lack the divergence that is the foundation of a multi-faceted reporting. You can ensure that you create that diversity in the news you read. Consider multiple sources, remain open-minded. Creating such diversity is a challenge in our times of social media bubbles. It takes an effort to be in contact with others of different opinions. This is a muscle you can train, and the longer you train and practice, the more you will help develop the muscle of others, too. And little by little you will help strengthening our democracies.

It is important to ask open questions when you inquire about things. How we perceive reality has a great influence in how we relate to others and how we react to information. Our worldview influences what we value and prioritize and what we tend to ignore or sacrifice; it reflects on how we engage with the present and the future. Let us be mindful that our ability to recognize what we think is right may not be right. Italian quantum physicist, Carlo Rovelli, suggests that the search for knowledge must not be based on certainty; it needs to be based on a radical distrust in certainty.[6] If our beliefs represent our bets on the future and, hence, influence our intentions and actions, we need to pay attention to who drives the background conversation in our head.[7] We risk intellectual isolation otherwise.

The antidote to intellectual isolation is to seek intellectual diversity. Go out of your way to seek out different points of view. Encourage opinions that make you feel uncomfortable. Seek out thought leaders that unsettle you, that appear weird or unorthodox. Remind yourself that if everybody around you appears to agree with you, there is something fundamentally flawed in your world. And do not get comfortable by thinking that you are in a diverse field just because you are surrounded by those of different age, gender, or origin. If you generally agree with people that offer a visual diversity, it does not mean that you are in a group that reflect a mental diversity. Diversity of opinion means diversity of opinion. A good manner to approach it is to ask yourself: What can I learn from this conversation, and how differently do I emerge?

I would like to close with an appeal. Let us all be conscious about our own biases and let us be more courageous in engaging with people who hold different opinions and perspectives and who may even live in different realities. Let us hear, feel, and experience divergent opinions. Let us have the courage to admit that we may not know it all. Let us be the ones who create a space where others can express themselves without feeling judged. Let us dare to create and hold spaces where such divergent views can be discussed without forcing a conclusion. Dialogue is the magic tool here. Let us see the other, connect with the other. Let us be the bridge builders that are needed so that we can overcome polarization in our journey to co-create a world that is worth living in for all of us, not just a select few of us. Our democracies and as a result our societies and all living beings depend on it.

Notes

1 Muff, K. (ed.) (2014): *The Collaboratory – A Co-creative Stakeholder Engagement Process for Solving Complex Problems*. Sheffield: Greenleaf Publishing.
2 Muff, K. (2018): *Five Superpowers for Co-creators*. Routledge. www.5superpowers.org
3 Rauch, J. (2021): *The Constitution of Knowledge – A Defense of Truth*. Washington, DC: Brookings Institution Press.
4 Papathomas, L., and Kuhn, D. (2017). Learning to argue via apprenticeship. *Journal of Experimental Child Psychology*, 159, 129–139: https://doi.org/10.1016/j.jecp.2017.01.013
5 O'Connor, C., and Weatherall, J.O. (2018): *The Misinformation Age – How False Beliefs Spread*. New Haven: Yale University Press.
6 Rovelli, C. (2015): *Seven Brief Lessons on Physics*. Translated by Carnell, S. and Segre, E. Great Britain: Penguin Books.
7 O'Brien, K. (2020): You matter more than you think – Quantum social change in response to a world in crisis: www.youmattermorethanyouthink.com/

Bibliography

Beck, D.E., and Cowan, C.C. (2005): *Spiral Dynamics: Mastering Values, Leadership and Change*. Chichester: John Wiley and Sons Ltd.

Bohm, D. (1993): The Undivided Universe: An Ontological Interpretation of Quantum Theory. Published Post-Humously.

Brodnig, I. (2021): *Einspruch! Verschwörungsmythen und Fake News kontern – in der Familie, im Freudeskreis und online*. Wien: Brandstätter.

Brown, B. (2017): *Braving the Wilderness*. New York: Ebury Publishing.

Cialdini, R. (2007): *Influence – The Psychology of Persuasion*. New York: Harper Collins Publishing.

De Smet, A., Dowling, B., Mugayar-Baldocchi, M., and Schaninger, B. (2021): *'Great Attrition' or 'Great Attraction'? The Choice Is Yours*. McKinsey Quarterly. Accessed online August 28, 2022: https://www.mckinsey.com/business-functions/people-and-organizational-performance/our-insights/great-attrition-or-great-attraction-the-choice-is-yours

Dutton, K. (2011): *Split-Second Persuasion: The Ancient Art & New Science of Changing Minds*. Boston, MA: Houghton Mifflin.

Dyllick, T., and Muff, K. (2016): Clarifying the meaning of sustainable business – Introducing a typology from business-as-usual to true business sustainability. *Organization & Environment*. Vol. 29, 156–174.

Eigenmann D. (2021): Die Mehrheit der Deutschen fühlt sich gegängelt. *Tagesanzeiger*, June 24. Accessed online July 4, 2021: https://epaper.tagesanzeiger.ch/#article/20/Tages%2DAnzeiger/2021-06-24/4/123611291

European Citizen Assemblies: https://citizensassemblies.org/european/

Flüglister, L. (2021): 60 Prozent Hatten Schon Streit wegen Umgang mit Corona. *SRG-Corona-Monitor*, July 23: www.srf.ch/news/schweiz/srg-corona-monitor-60-prozent-hatten-schon-streit-wegen-umgang-mit-corona?wt_mc_o=srf.share.app.srf-app.email

Fromme, C., and Wichert, S. (2021): Menschen werden eher aktiv, wenn es den persönlichen Interessen dient. *Tages Anzeiger*, September 25: https://epaper.tagesanzeiger.ch/#article/20/Tages%2DAnzeiger/2021-09-25/35/125131036

Gardner, H. (2006): *Changing Minds*. Boston, MA: Harvard Business Review Press.

Gasteiger, C., and Mayer, V. (2021): Immer mehr Journalisten wollen nicht objektiv sein. *Tagesanzeiger*, March 30. Accessed online July 4, 2021: https://epaper.tagesanzeiger.ch/#article/20/Tages%2D Anzeiger/2021-03-30/12/121408279

Isaacs, W. (2021): Accessing genuine dialogue. *The Watercooler – Straight Talk on Strategic Issues*. Vol. 6 (4), July/August 2012, 9–11: www.watercoolernewsletter.com

Jackson Rainer, J. (2019): Five Ways to Have a Civil Conversation in a Polarized Society. *Next Avenue*, February 9, 2019. Accessed online August 28, 2022: https://www.marketwatch.com/story/5-ways-to-have-a-civil-conversation-in-a-polarized-society-2019-02-05

Jay, J., and Grant, G. (2017): *Breaking through Gridlock – The Power of Conversation in a Polarized World*. Oakland: Berret-Köhler.

Kalmoe, N.P., and Mason, L. (2019): Lethal Mass Partisanship: Prevalence, Correlates, and Electroal Contingencies. Contribution to the NCAPSA American Politics Meeting, Washington, DC, January. Accessed online May 4, 2021: www.dannyhayes.org/uploads/6/9/8/5/69858539/kalmoe___mason_ncapsa_2019_-_lethal_partisanship_-_final_lmedit.pdf

Klein, E. (2020): *Why We're Polarized*. London: Profile Books.

Kuhn-Spogat, I. (2021): Green-running. CEOs vor! Das "Green Business CEO"-Rating bewertet erstmals nicht nur Facts & Figures zur Nachhaltigkeit, sondern stellt die CEOs ins Rampenlicht. *Bilanz Zeitschrift*, June 30: www.handelszeitung.ch/bilanz/green-running

Langer, M.-A. (2020): Die Amerikaner gehen in die Selbsttherapie. *NZZ*, December 27. Accessed online August 3, 2021: www.nzz.ch/international/graeben-in-den-usa-amerikaner-gehen-in-selbsttherapie-ld.1593051?reduced=true

Langer, M.-A. (2021): We Are Much Dumber Than We Like to Think. *NZZ*, August 17: www.nzz.ch/english/social-media-spreads-misinformation-berkeley-researcher-says-ld.1638804

Leadership for Transition, a EU-Funded Multi-Phase Research Project: http://leadership-for-transition.eu/?page_id=36

Maoz, I. (2000): An Experiment in Peace: Reconciliation-Aimed Workshops of Jewish-Israeli and Palestinian Youth. *Journal of Peace Research*. Vol. 37–6, 721–736.

McArdle, M. (2015): *The Upside of Down: Why Failing Well Is the Key to Success*. New York: Penguin Publishing Group.

Muff, K. (ed.) (2014): *The Collaboratory – A Co-creative Stakeholder Engagement Process for Solving Complex Problems*. Sheffield: Greenleaf Publishing.

Muff, K. (2019): *Five Superpowers for Co-creators – How Change Makers and Business Can Achieve the Sustainable Development Goals*. Sheffield: Routledge.

Muff, K. (2021): Positive Impact Innovation. *Sustainability*. Vol. 13 (16), 8891: www.mdpi.com2071-105013168891

Muff, K., Liechti, A., and Dyllick, T. (2020): How to Apply Responsible Leadership Theory in Practice – A Competency Tool to Collaborate on the Sustainable Development Goals. *Corporate*

Social Responsibility and Environment CSRaEM Journal. Vol. 27–5, 2254–2274.
O'Brien, K. (2020): You Matter More Than You Think – Quantum Social Change in Response to a World in Crisis: www.youmattermorethanyouthink.com/
O'Connor, C., and Weatherall, J.O. (2018): *The Misinformation Age – How False Beliefs Spread*. New Haven: Yale University Press.
Papathomas, L., and Kuhn, D. (2017): Learning to Argue Via Apprenticeship. *Journal of Experimental Child Psychology*. Vol. 159, 129–139. doi: 10.1016/j.jecp.2017.01.013
Polman, P. (2021): Infliction Points for Senior Leaders. Video Interview in Wendepunkt by Dennis Shuler: www.kineticconsulting.com/2021/02/wendepunkt-inflection-points-for-senior-leaders-with-paul-polman/
Precht, R.D. (2021): *Von der Pflicht. Eine Betrachtung*. Munich: Wilhelm Goldmann Verlag.
Rauch, J. (2021): *The Constitution of Knowledge – A Defense of Truth*. Washington, DC: Brookings Institution Press.
Ribi, T. (2021): Warum sind Autokraten so attraktiv? *NZZ Feuilleton*, March 30. Accessed online July 5, 2021: www.nzz.ch/feuilleton/was-macht-autokraten-attraktiv-anne-applebaum-sucht-antworten-id.1608885
Ries, T.E. (2020): The 2021 Edelman Trust Barometer. Accessed online August 28, 2022: www.edelman.com/trust/2021-trust-barometer
Ries, T.E. (2021): The 2022 Edelman Trust Barometer. Accessed online August 28, 2022: www.edelman.com/trust/2022-trust-barometer
Rimanoczy, I. (2020): *The Sustainability Mindset Principles – A Guide to Developing a Mindset for a Better World*. London; New York: Routledge.
Rovelli, C. (2015): *Seven Brief Lessons on Physics*. Translated by Carnell, S., and Segre, E. Great Britain: Penguin Books.
Schumacher Cohen, J. (2019): Polarized World Dialogue – Radical Act. *American Magazine*, December 3: www.americamagazine.org/politics-society/2019/12/03/polarized-world-dialogue-radical-act
Segatori, S. (2017): What Is Integral Philosophy, Integral Theory? Extract from the "Integral Center Membership Manual" in Boulder Colorado: https://medium.com/@ssegatori/what-is-integral-philosophy-integral-theory-5c6b0ccc7724
Shafak, E. (2020): *How to Stay Sane in an Age of Division*. London: Wellcome Collection.
Sunstein, C.R. (2002): The Law of Group Polarization. *The Journal of Political Philosophy*. Vol. 10–2, 175–195.
Taber, C.S., and Lodge, M. (2006): Motivated Skepticism in the Evaluation of Political Beliefs. *American Journal of Political Science*. Vol. 50–3, 755–769
Vox Pro: www.civinc.co/about
Widmer, B. (2021): Wieso sorgt die Pandemie für derart viele Konflikte? *SRG-Corona-Monitor*, July 23: www.srf.ch/news/schweiz/srg-corona-monitor-60-prozent-hatten-schon-streit-wegen-umgang-mit-corona?wt_mc_o=srf.share.app.srf-app.email

Young, J. (2020): The Art of Communication in a Polarized World. *Journal of Cultural Analysis and Social Change*. Vol. 5 (2), 16: https://doi.org/10.20897/jcasc/9326

Ziblatt, D., and Levitsky, S. (2021): The Despair of the Old Majority: American Conservatives Risk the Democracy. *Wissenschaftszentrum Berlin für Sozialforschung (WZB) Mitteilungen*. (17), 6–9.

Index

Page numbers in **bold** refer to figures.

For Product Safety Concerns and Information please contact our EU representative GPSR@taylorandfrancis.com Taylor & Francis Verlag GmbH, Kaufingerstraße 24, 80331 München, Germany